MARINE JOURNAL.
PORT OF NANTUCKET.

Monday, Jan 28th.
ARRIVED.
Steamer Telegraph, New Bedford.
Tuesday, Jan 29th
SAILED.
Steamer Telegraph, N. Bedford

MEMORANDA.

Ard at Mattapoisett Jan 27, brig Annawan, Taber, South Atlantic Ocean, with full cargo, 550 bbls sp oil. Spoke Oct 29, lat 16 50 S, lon 36 19 W, barks Dove, Forsyth, NL, clean, for Indian Ocean; Nov 3, lat 17 50 lon 36 50, Chase, Ricketson, NB, 100 sp on board, for California; 16th, lat 16 26 lon 36 10, Rainbow, of and fm Baltimore for Rio Janeiro; 20th, lat 16 58 lon 36 20, Mattapoisett, Wing, Westport, 230 sp; 22d, lat 17 20, lon 36 10, ship Susan, Howland, NB, clean, Capt sick; Dec 4, lat 17 25, lon 36 40, sch R C White, 31 ds fm Baltimore for San Francisco; 5th, lat 17 53 lon 36 56, brig Zoroaster, Handy, 52 ds fm NB, for San Francisco; on Abrolhos Banks Dec 7, lat 17 4 lon 37 4, brig Gov. Hopkins, Baker, Dartmouth, 180 sp; 12th, lat 16 57 lon 36 58, barks Exchange, Hazard, NB, clean; 13th, lat 16 39 lon 37, Dr Franklin, Gifford, Westport, 280 sp; hd fm same date, President, Sowle, do, 100 sp on board; Barclay, King, do, 200 sp

Sld fm Greenport 19th, brig Pioneer, (new whaler, 235 tons,) Weeks, S Atlantic Ocean.

At Sydney, N. S. W, in September, ship Harrison, Sherman, NB, for San Francisco—had shipped her oil to London.

Sld from Zanzibar Oct 10, Phenix, Bloomfield, NL, 120 bbls sp oil; 11th, Columbia, Andrews, do, 240 sp 80 wh.

Sld fm N York Jan 28, steamship Southerner, Berry, Charleston.

Cld at Philadelphia 25th sch Jacob Raymond. Bourne, Charleston.

Ar at Norfolk 22d, sch Bolivar, Barnard, Georgetown, SC, for this port.

Ship Neptune, of Sagharbor, and Eliza Thornton, of New York, have been purchased in New Bedford, supposed for the California trade.

Letters recd in town from ship Fanny, of this port, for California, rept her, Oct 30, lat 11 41 S, lon 34 09 W, all well.

A letter fm Capt Brush, of ship Golconda, of NB, dated Paita Dec 16, states that he had nearly recovered his health, and would leave in a short time for Callao, to rejoin his ship, which was then cruising in charge of the mate.

A letter fm Capt Little, of ship Emma C Jones of NB, repts her at Fayal Dec 17, with 191 bbls sp oil, to be shipped home.

A letter fm Mr. Wm P. Grinnell, dated on board bark Pantheon, Price, NB, at sea, Dec 18, lat 24 N, lon 28 W, all well on board, for San Francisco.

SPOKEN.

At sea, Nov 19, no lat &c., bark John A. Robb, Wimpenny, Fii, for Pacific Ocean, all well.

July 20, lat 37 1-2 lon 70, brig Rodman, Bowen, fm NB, via N York, for Rio Grande and California.

DISASTERS.

Ship Vicksburg, Berry, from New Orleans, at New York, reports Jan 25, at 3.30 A M, Sandy Hook bearing NNW 60 miles, came in contact with the propeller Sea Gull from New York for California—carrying away all our head yards, main yard and foretop gallant mast; tearing away the larboard fore channels, fore shrouds and foretopmast backstays, staving in rail and breaking several stanchions; also tore away lower studding sail and boom, and split foretopsail and mainsail all to pieces.

Propeller Sea Gull, Cessery, from New York for California, on the 25th, at 4 o'clock in the morning, when 65 miles SE of the Hook was run into by the ship Vicksburg, the Sea Gull being on the wind at the time, which carried away the Sea Gull's three topmasts, head of the main and foremasts, mainyard, main topsail, and all the rigging attached, carried away bowsprit, jibboom, stove in larboard bow from the cat head to the fore rigging and down to the plank shear. The Sea Gull was towed to New York, 26th inst, to repair damages.

Telegraphic reports from New Orleans, to the 24th inst, state that the steamer Ohio, from Havana, whilst going up the river, came in collision with the

NOTICE TO MARINERS.
NEW LIGHT HOUSE.

On and after the 1st day of February, 1850, there will be shown from Sankaty Head, on the S. E. part of the Island of NANTUCKET, a new Light, bearing South by West twenty three miles from the Light Vessel on Pollock Rip, and South by East nine miles from the fixed White Light on the extremity of Great Point, Nantucket.

The NEW LIGHT will be a FIXED WHITE LIGHT WITH BRILLIANT WHITE FLASHES: two successive flashes being given at intervals of one and a half minute, then the third flash at an interval of three minutes, followed by two successive flashes at intervals of one and a half minute, then a third flash at an interval of three minutes as before, and so on for the time that the Light is visible. The FIXED Light will not be visible farther than 12 or 15 miles, beyond which the flashes only will be seen.

The Light is projected by a revolving Lenticular Apparatus of the 2d order.

The centre of the Light will be 15 feet above the level of the sea, and the FLASHES will be visible as far as this elevation and the state of atmospheric refraction permit.

The Light Tower is 70 feet high from base to top of Lantern, and will be painted in three rings horizontally: the top and bottom rings being white, the middle ring red.

WM. R. EASTON, Collector.
Nantucket, Dec. 24th, 1849.—1F1

NANTUCKET LIGHTS

AN
ILLUSTRATED HISTORY
OF THE ISLAND'S
LEGENDARY BEACONS

KAREN T. BUTLER

Mill Hill Press

Nantucket, Massachusetts

1996

Mill Hill Press
124 Orange Street
Nantucket, Massachusetts 02554

Library of Congress Catalog No. 96-094744
ISBN 0-9638910-6-5

A portion of the proceeds from sale of this book will benefit the Nantucket Life Saving Museum.

Cover photograph: Sankaty Head Lighthouse in 1904
Endpapers: *The Nantucket Inquirer,* February 4, 1850

This book is dedicated

with great affection to my husband

Tony Cahill, the light of my life,

in appreciation for many a

runtum scoot *

around this hallowed island,

Nantucket

*An old Nantucket term referring to an excursion, usually a drive but possibly on foot,

undertaken with or without destination but most definitely for pleasure's sake.

NANTUCKET

0   1   2   3   4
Miles

MUSKEGET

TUCKERNUCK

NANTUCKET SOUND

Great Point Light

Chord of the Bay

GREAT PO

Brant Point Light

N

W   E

S

Smith Point

ESTHER ISLAND

Eel Point

EEL POINT ROAD

Warren Landing

Madaket Harbor

Dionis Beach
Capaum Pond

North Head of Long Pond

Massy Ponds

Washing Pond

CLIFF RD

Jetties Beach

Coatue Point

First Pt

Abrams Pt

Second Pt

Life Saving Museum

Quaise

Bass Pt

Pocom

Five Fingered Pt.

Third Pt.

Brant Point

Pinny's Pt.

Nantucket

Nantucket Harbor

FUDGE HILL

SHAWKEMO HILLS

POLPIS ROAD

Monomoy

Madaket

MADAKET RD.

Head of Hummock

Hither Creek

Long Pond

Hummock Pond

HUMMOCK POND ROAD

VESPER LANE

MADAKET ROAD

OLD SOUTH ROAD

MILESTONE

NOBADEER RD

Cisco

Mioxes Pond

Miacomet Pond

SURFSIDE RD

ATLANTIC AVENUE

Nantucket Memorial Airport

Madequecham

Surfside

Miacomet Rip

EAST JETTY

WEST JETTY

Drawn by
GEORGE BUCTEL
Researched, designed, and produced by
HENRY MITCHELL HAVEMEYER
of Nantucket
Research assistant
RICHARD P. SWAIN
of Nantucket

MITCHELLS
BOOK CORNER

PUBLISHED AND COPYRIGHTED BY
MITCHELL'S BOOK CORNER
54 MAIN STREET
NANTUCKET, MASS. 02554
© COPYRIGHT 1973

Original Terminal on Steamboat Wharf, 1881

Bark "W. F. Marshall" ashore near
Mioxes Pond, March 9, 1877

Contents

Color section follows page 58

Beacon Lights

When I am cowardly, sick of the fight,

Dumb for the right word, nerveless for deeds that dare,

Blaze up in my heart, square little Brant Point Light;

Light me a broad path starred with a burnished flare!

If I am tossing on a sea of doubt,

And have no harbor, no fair shore to know,

Sankaty, like an angel, spread your great wings out,

Headland and coastal light, give me your glow!

If I am lost and waves go over me,

Tossing, engulfing hollows o'er my head;

Thou, Great Point Light, will surely cover me,

And by thy strong white clue I shall be led!

When I am caught in foam of treacherous beach,

And all the darkness presses like a wall,

Blaze, Island lights, beyond the Island reach;

Beacon me to the Utmost Light of all!

—Edwina Stanton Babcock (1924)

Great Point and lighthouse in 1963.

Preface

For the sea is his; he owns it, as Emperors own empires . . . .

—Herman Melville, on the Nantucketer, in

Moby-Dick (1851)

Stars twinkle in the clear Nantucket night. The tiny lights of fishing boats in search of their daily catch dot the horizon. The beams of Brant Point, Great Point, and Sankaty Head lighthouses slowly traverse the skies, signaling the island's presence to ships at sea. The ghostlike beam of the Nantucket South Shoals Light Vessel, long since gone from her sentinel post, can be imagined bobbing and rolling above the treacherous Nantucket shoals.

Perhaps the appeal of lighthouses is that those beacons beaming over the water suggest hope and trust. A lighthouse standing on the shore evokes both the dedication of the lightkeeper and the faith of the mariner in that keeper's steadfast vigilance. Whatever the weather—foggy, stormy, or calm—the lightkeeper was always alert to the perils that might befall his counterpart, the mariner, at sea. The life of a keeper might be considered mundane, even boring; yet on occasion it could be adventurous, and sometimes even dangerous.

Gone are the lightkeepers of Nantucket; their time grows more distant in our memories with each passing year. *Nantucket Lights* endeavors to capture the essence of their lives and the colorful history of the beacons they maintained. This history, not embellished but rather retold as truthfully as many memories can recreate it, may

The self-sufficient building cluster at Sankaty Head. Fuel, supplies, and even a few cows could be kept at the lighthouse.

shed its own light upon a small but important segment of Nantucket's maritime heritage.

Although the lighthouses at Brant Point, Great Point, and Sankaty Head have similar functions, each has always had its unique characteristics. Some of this uniqueness is strictly practical: if a light is not immediately identifiable, mariners can misjudge their location and risk serious consequences; the distinctive features of lighthouses and lightships are part of the visual language that guides mariners along their route, safe from danger. Seamen studying charts understand this language: the timing and color of each flash distinguish one light from another, in hundreds of permutations; the color markings of a distant lighthouse tower tell its name as if in block letters; the color, sound, and set of buoys speak of channels, obstructions, and currents.

Equally distinctive were the beacons of the lightships that once protected shipping along much of America's coastline. These sturdy vessels, built with the buoyancy of cork and the durability of rock, were moored at sea in some of the most terrifyingly unpredictable waters anywhere in the world, shining their lights in all conditions and bearing the men who manned them through extraordinary hardship and risk.

Lighthouses and lightships are built to withstand heavy weather and turbulent seas, though some of Nantucket's early structures were not all that durable. Nature takes its toll on the lighthouses on the island: fierce storms and inevitable erosion have caused some of Nantucket's shoreline to slip away forever, taking at least one lighthouse—Great Point—and placing another—Sankaty Head—in jeopardy.

A succession of diminutive Nantucket lightships at their exposed sea-post to the south-southeast of the island were also subjected to the pounding of the mighty Atlantic Ocean. But they were sturdy vessels with valorous crews, and so they held their position on the Nantucket South Shoals until modern technology made them obsolete.

Extinction of the manned lightship came swiftly, as transatlantic vessels grew in size and weight, posing a real threat to the crews of the much smaller lightships. The potential for loss of life and the expense of building new "unsinkable" lightships eventually proved to be far more costly than setting and maintaining unmanned buoys housing highly reliable, advanced technology.

Children enjoy a picnic on scenic Sankaty bluff in 1906, with the lightkeeper's Victorian-style dwelling in the background.

Bookplate issued by the United States Lighthouse Establishment.

The same advances in electronic navigational technology also led to automated on-shore beacons that ended the need for traditional lighthouses manned by lightkeepers along the Atlantic seaboard. Picturesque, eternal symbols of security and trust (one New England bank used a lighthouse as its symbol for decades), today these beacons are the object of restoration efforts and the stuff of legend.

The keepers of Nantucket's legendary beacons are the heart and soul of this story. We may have a romantic image of a lighthouse keeper with his wife beside him, pondering the oceanic vista before his isolated, picturesque home. His gaze is noble, clear, all-encompassing; his thoughts are as deep and eternal as the sea.

In fact, even on the picturesque island of Nantucket, lighthouse and lightship life was often routine, wearing, and dull. The keeper's time was taken up with boring and repetitive tasks, and his attention was fully absorbed in making certain that the light functioned properly. The physical demands of the job were endless, making a social life more often than not out of the question. This was especially true at the remote stations of Great Point and Sankaty; Brant Point, being so close to town, offered far more opportunities for socializing. The most isolated duty of all was aboard the Nantucket South Shoals Lightship, whose crewmembers treasured their infrequent shore leave.

Even though lighthouses occupy some of the most spectacular locations along America's coast, lightkeepers did not necessarily seek their jobs for the pleasure of being near the water. In storms or on the blackest nights, the light had to be lit, and often enough the keeper had no idea whether even a single mariner was at sea to look for it. Maintaining the light was a sacred trust, and the discipline of the job—and the legal and moral ramifications of dereliction of duty—was extreme. In theory, the keeper's job was only to maintain and operate the light; rescue was not part of the duty. (A keeper was not charged with the responsibility for saving people, but if a ship went aground on the shore near his light, he was to alert others to come to the rescue.) A keeper was not expected to sit up all night watching the light; once it was lighted, he went to bed. In the days before elec-trification, however, the keeper might haul himself out of bed and climb the tower stairs at regular inter-vals throughout the night to check or relight the light. Occasionally, as the wick burned down, the light would begin to fail and sometimes went out. In the 1870s a device was developed that rang a bell, signal-ing that the light was going out. After a demanding night, there was still much work to be done—polish-

Brant Point in 1948. This shot is part of the Coast Guard's thorough record of their installations on Nantucket Island.

A very young Bob Caldwell poses with his mother in front of Brant Point Lighthouse in 1926.

ing, cleaning, refueling, repairing—throughout the next day. Until the innovative Fresnel lens was brought to the United States in the 1850s, a lighthouse was essentially a one-man operation. Later, more complex lights were regulated by clockworks that required periodic winding. In addition, the intricate system of Fresnel lenses required a maintenance schedule that one man could not handle, and assistant keepers were hired to share the responsibilities.

The conveniences of electricity and plumbing did not become standard in lighthouses until after World War II. The pay was always modest. Yet, despite all the discomforts and inconveniences of the work, the position of lightkeeper was eagerly sought, especially in the nineteenth century. In many coastal communities at that time there were few jobs that offered regular wages or security of any kind. Some men were tradesmen or farmers; many were sailors, dependent for their living on the demand for their services. As an employee of the federal government, a lighthouse keeper had a monthly paycheck and a guaranteed roof over his family's head.

The life of a keeper's wife was in many ways even more arduous than her husband's. In addition to caring for her family in a home with few household amenities, she usually had to help her husband with his routine chores. Furthermore, most lighthouses were so remote that she was deprived of friends and neighbors close by. Strong ties did exist among lightkeeping families, however, and they kept abreast of one another's activities and shared their experiences and news of local events.

Many of the keepers and their wives stayed on the job until they were well on in years, devoting nearly their entire lives to caring for the lights. Even with all the hardships, they seemed to have enjoyed what they did.

The first system of lighthouses in America started in New England. Heavy maritime traffic and rough, variable weather conditions in the North Atlantic created a need for a system of navigational aids. Furthermore, it was in the economic interest of coastal communities like Nantucket to create safe pathways to their harbors. (It has also been alleged that some more isolated communities found it in *their* interest to

The steamship Naushon *outbound past Brant Point Lighthouse in the early 1930s.*

16

LIGHTS OF THE UNITED STATES.

MASSACHUSETTS.

Number.		Name.	Location.	Latitude north.	Longitude west.	Number of lights and relative positions.	Fog-signal.
82		Nauset Beach, (Beacons)............	Three towers and lights at Eastham, on the east side of Cape Cod, Mass.	41 51 37	69 56 44	1 } 150 feet apart, N. and S.	
83		....				1 }	
84		....				1 }	
85		Chatham................................	On the Main, west side of Chatham harbor, Mass., Nauset beach being on the east side.	41 40 15	69 56 37	1 } 70 feet apart, N. and S.	
86		....				1 }	
87		Pollock Rip Light-vessel............	Off Chatham, 4 miles E. ½ S. of Monomy light-house.	41 32 (07)	69 54 (48)	1	A bell, horn, and gun.
88	EAST ENTRANCE TO VINEYARD SOUND.	Monomoy Point.....................	On Monomoy beach, the southern extremity of Cape Cod, Mass.	41 33 32	69 59 17	1	
89		Shovelful Shoals Light-vessel......	Off Chatham, 2¼ miles S. SW. ¼ W. from Monomoy Point light-house.	41 32 (14)	69 59 (15)	1	A bell, horn, and gun..
90		Handkerchief Light-vessel	Off the southern point of the Handkerchief shoal, in Vineyard sound, Mass.	41 39 (36)	70 03 (20)	1	A bell, horn, and gun..
91		NANTUCKET, (Great Point)..........	On Sandy or Great point, the northeast extremity of Nantucket island.	41 23 22	70 02 25	1	
92		SANKATY HEAD.....................	On the southeast extremity of the island of Nantucket, about S. by W., 23 miles from Pollock Rip lightvessel.	41 16 59	69 57 35	1	
93		Nantucket New South Shoals Lightvessel.	Placed about 2 miles south of the southern extremity of Davis's New South shoal, off Nantucket, in 14 fathoms water.	40 56 (00)	69 51 (30)	2	A bell, horn, and gun..
94		GAY HEAD................................	On the western point of Martha's Vineyard island.	41 20 52	70 49 47	1	
95	VINEYARD SOUND.	Brant Point........................	On Brant point, entrance to Nantucket harbor, Mass.	41 17 77	70 05 15	1 }	
96		Nantucket Range Beacon.....	On the rising ground, about 1 mile in the rear of Brant Point lighthouse.	......	......	1 }	
97		Nantucket Cliff Range Beacon, (front.)	On the beach northwest of Nantucket harbor, Mass.	......	......	1 } 300 feet apart, NW. and SE.	
98		Range Beacon, (rear)............	....			1 }	

Nantucket lights as listed in the 1863 "List of the Lights of the United States." The "Cliff Beacons" (number 79) were also known as the Bug Lights.

LIGHTS OF THE UNITED STATES. 17

MASSACHUSETTS.

Number.	Fixed or revolving, &c.	Time between flashes.	Distance visible, in nautical miles.	Color of tower or vessel.	Height of tower from base to focal plane.	Height of light above sea level.	Order of lens.	When established.	When last rebuilt.	When last refitted.	Compass range of visibility.	Remarks.
		m. s.										
82	F		15	White	20	93	[⊙ 6]	1837		1856	N. 4 W. by E'd to S.	Three circular brick towers, whitewashed; lanterns black. Abreast of these lights the tides divide and run in opposite directions.
83	F			White			[⊙ 6]					
84	F			White			[⊙ 6]					
85	F		14	White	40	70	[⊙ 4]	1808		1857	N. 19 E. by E'd to S. 26 W.	Two circular towers, whitewashed; lanterns black. Pollock Rip light-vessel bears S.; east end of broken ground of Pollock Rip bears S. by E.
86	F			White			[⊙ 4]					
87	F		12	Red	30	45	Refls.	1849	1868	1868	Entire horizon	Reflector light; one red hoop-iron day-mark at the masthead, with POLLOCK RIP painted in large white letters on each side. A north course (mag.) from near this vessel, if made good, will take a vessel through the slue in three fathoms at low tide. There is a buoy bearing N. by E. from the vessel, distant half a mile.
88	F		12	Red	30	41	[⊙ 4]	1823		1857	N. 33 E. by E'd to N. 13 E.	Cast-iron tower, painted red; lantern black. This and the Chatham lights serve to guide vessels in going through the north channel on the south side of the cape, passing north of Handkerchief and Bishop and Clerk's. This light, bearing NW. by W. ¼ W. will take a vessel in or out clear of Pollock Rip.
89	F		12	Green	28	40	Refls.	1852		1855	Entire horizon	Reflector light; one red hoop-iron day-mark at masthead. This vessel lies west from Pollock Rip light-vessel, and has SHOVELFUL painted in large white letters on each side. There is a red buoy near it, on the point of the Shovelful shoal.
90	F		12	Straw	28	40	Refls.	1855			Entire horizon	Reflector light. Schooner rigged, painted straw color, with HANDKERCHIEF painted in large black letters on each side. Two hoop-iron day-marks, one at each masthead, painted black.
91	F		14	White	60	70	[⊙ 3]	1784*		1857	S. 22 E. by W'd to S. 35 E.	Whitewashed stone tower, lantern black. Good anchorage inside the point, in easterly weather, in 7 and 8 fathoms water.
92	F. V. F.	1.00	19	White, red, and white.	65	150	[⊙ 2]	1849			N. 74 W. by E'd to S. 16 W.	This light shows a brilliant flash of 10 seconds' duration once in every minute, and a fixed light during the remaining 50 seconds, within the range of visibility of the fixed light. Cape Cod light 47 miles, and Gay Head light 39 miles, distant from this light.
93	2 F		12	Red	34	44	Refls.	1856	1869		Entire horizon	Two reflector lights. Magnetic bearings from light-vessel to Old South shoal, N. by E., distant 8 miles. Tom Never's Head, N. NW. ¼ W., distant 21 miles. Block Island light, W. NW., distant 78 miles. Sandy Hook light-vessel, W., distant 180 miles. This light-vessel is schooner-rigged, has two hoop-iron day-marks (one at each masthead) painted red. Hull painted red, with the words "Nantucket Shoals," in white letters, on each side.
94	Flg	0.10	20	Red	41	170	[⊙ 1]	1799	1856		S. 32 E. by W'd to N. 86 E.	A guide to Vineyard sound and Buzzard's bay, 39 miles from Sankaty Head light, 48 miles from Montauk Point light, and 30 miles from Point Judith. A rocky shoal, distant 1¼ mile, lies northwest from this light. Cuttyhunk island bears N. 45° W., distant 7¼ miles. "Vineyard Sound" light-vessel distant about 7 miles.
95	F		12	Red	42	46	[⊙ 4]	1759*	1856		N. 56 W. by E'd to S. 53 W.	This tower, in range with Nantucket beacon, will clear Black flat, leaving the shoal on the starboard hand.
96	F		5	White	6	10	Refl.	1794*	1869			Light shown from a small wooden building in the rear of Brant point, and on the south side of the harbor, to serve as a range with the main light.
97	F		4	White		8	Refl.	1838		1856		There are two small pyramidal wooden structures, NW. by W. ¼ (mag.) from Brant Point light. The following are correct guides for entering the harbor of Nantucket:
98	F		4			10	Refl.	1838		1856		Bring the Cliff beacon-lights (red and white) in range, and run for them, passing near the bell buoy in three fathoms water; keep on this course until up with the red buoy No. 2 on the outer bar. The course on this range is SW. ¼ S.; then steer for Brant Point light, S. by E., passing the red buoys Nos. 4 and 6; then for Red Cliff beacon-light, SW. by S. ¼ S., until the rear beacon and Brant Point lights are in range; then steer on this range, passing the red buoys, (outer, middle, and inner Black flat buoys, Nos. 8, 10, and 12.) The course on this range will be SE. by S. ¼ S., passing Brant point within 100 fathoms, and then steer SW. for the anchorage, in from two to three fathoms, soft bottom. Courses magnetic,

Atlantic——3

lure ships to their doom by establishing false beacons along dangerous stretches of shoreline, and then stripping the wrecks. These so-called "moon-cussers" have their own place in the annals of lights and lighthouses, but the Quaker ethic—human beings taken care of first—was strong on Nantucket. The island is emphatically *not* a part of the moon-cusser story.)

The original thirteen colonies each established lighthouses to satisfy local needs. As one of its earliest actions, the new Congress passed an act on August 7, 1789, assuming responsibility for all lighthouses then in operation, with a commitment to build new ones. The lighthouse system was placed within the Treasury Department under the Commissioner of Revenue, where it remained until the creation of the Lighthouse Board in 1852.

That lighthouses were originally in the Treasury's domain may seem strange. For many years, the government of the young republic depended on customs duties paid on imported goods for much of its revenue. Obviously, the Treasury had a vested interest in shipping safety in order to guarantee receipt of appropriate revenue from vessels coming into American ports.

In 1851 Congress conducted an investigation of the nation's lighthouse system in the wake of mounting complaints about its inadequacy and inefficiency. The investigation revealed that the lighthouse establishment was largely an insider group that controlled the purchase of equipment and the building of light-

houses, primarily for their own profit. Driven by self-interest, the insiders were content to retain the status quo rather than develop a first-rate lighthouse system. These individuals had few feelings of pride about lighthouses; it was their own greed that motivated them. They hired their cronies to build the lighthouses, and they arranged for the government to purchase lamp oil from their friends at inflated prices.

Even in light of all the damning evidence about the administration of lighthouses, the investigative board soft-pedaled its final report. Showing little interest in punishing wrongdoing, the panel instead maintained that it had "not sought so much to discover defects and point them out, as to show the necessity for a better system. Commerce and navigation, in which every citizen of this nation is interested, either directly or indirectly, claim it; the weather-beaten sailor asks it, and humanity demands it." The result was the creation of the Lighthouse Board, which oversaw the nation's lighthouses until 1910, when the board was replaced by the Lighthouse Service. In 1939 the Coast Guard became the keeper of the lights, a role it has played to the present.

The existence of a federal administrative structure for lighthouses did not provide much support for the individual lightkeeper; his own dedication was what kept the lights burning. Federal lighthouse inspectors did visit the lighthouses twice a year, awarding letters of commendation, not money, for a job well done. The keepers did strive to earn those marks of excellence from their superiors, fearing that any criticism would jeopardize their jobs. Inspectors traveled from lighthouse to lighthouse by Revenue Cutter (an armed Treasury vessel commissioned to monitor international trade), generally bringing wives along. The junkets usually took place in summer, and their great cost and paltry results played a part in creating the scandal that led to the review board of 1851.

Local political interests frequently determined the appointment of lightkeepers. On at least several occasions Nantucketers sent letters to the Lighthouse Board and the local newspaper, attempting to discredit a particular keeper's ability to mind the light. This forced the investigation of the keeper's competency. Often it was discovered that such attacks were merely maneuvers to replace the criticized keeper with one supported by the political faction in power at the time.

&

Nantucket's part in America's maritime history is an important one. As islanders dependent on the sea for their very existence, Nantucketers early on developed their seamanship skills to a high level. The island, an early observer wrote, was "a great nursery of seamen, pilots, coasters, and bank-fishermen; they often cross the sea to go to the main, and learn even in those short voyages how to qualify themselves for longer and more dangerous ones; they are therefore deservedly conspicuous for their maritime knowledge and experience, all over the continent."

Experience at sea was the Nantucketer's best teacher, although it could sometimes be a heartless one. Charts were few, and those that did exist were often inaccurate. Navigational knowledge was generally passed along by word of mouth. In 1769 Benjamin Franklin, for example, described gathering information from a Nantucket sea captain, his own distant cousin:

> *Captain Folger hath been so obliging as to mark for me on a chart the dimensions, course and swiftness of the* [Gulf Stream] *from its first coming out of the gulph* [of Mexico] *where it is narrowest and strongest, until it turns away to the southward of the western islands, where it is broader and weaker, and to give me withal some written directions whereby ships bound from the Banks of Newfoundland to New York may avoid the said stream; and yet be free of danger from the banks and shoals* [Cape Sable Shoals, Georges Bank, and the Nantucket Shoals].

The sea often brought tragedy as well as commerce to Nantucket's shores. Before the 1700s the maritime losses were small; islanders mostly fished close to shore in open boats and acquired their knowledge of local waters by trial and error. But economic need drove Nantucketers to venture farther off shore in search of trade, fish, and, most lucrative of all, whales. The risk increased, but, ironically, home waters remained among the most dangerous as ships'

Winter winds blow snow and sand across a cold, bleak Great Point.

drafts increased and the profit motive put a premium on haste. Hurricanes and Northeasters took their toll: homeward-bound islanders were shipwrecked and lost their lives on Nantucket's own shores.

During the period from 1750 to 1850 two out of five Nantucket mariners died at sea. Expensive ships, valuable cargo, and valiant sailors were being lost at a fearsome rate, and the waters around Nantucket were especially notorious. The increasing frequency of wrecks motivated the island's inhabitants, most of whom earned their livelihood from the sea, to take steps to make the lives of mariners more secure.

The development of the lighthouse system in the United States followed the same pattern it had in Europe, with the first lighthouses coming into service near important ports of trade. The sea was the high-way of the day, and the goal of government was to line this highway with lighthouses.

By 1830, Nantucket was the third largest sea-port in Massachusetts, after Boston and Salem. During the era when sailing ships dominated the seas, many used Nantucket Sound; up to fifteen hundred vessels a month passed by the island. Although this inshore passage was the most protected route along the New England coast, it was still subject to unpre-dictable gales, fog, and currents. The constantly altering shoals were also a menace to sailors, as tide rips with swift currents bored their way through the underwater sands. A few strategically placed buoys marked the constantly shifting channels, but those precautions were not enough to protect the mariners in all situations.

During the late 1700s and throughout the 1800s, ships from around the world made Nantucket a port of call, and even more passed close by the island. They were from Bombay, carrying cotton and spices; from North Carolina, with tar; from Havana carrying molasses; from Turk's Island in the Bahamas, bearing salt. The colorful list goes on and on, and so does the litany of loss. Many ships were wrecked totally, and an incalculable number suffered less crippling damage. Well over a thousand wrecks have been documented around the island of Nantucket, but the true number of shipwrecks off its coast will never be known.

Wrecks were not always as we think of them. Many ships would run aground with minor damage, quickly repaired. Some just went down in a storm, lost at sea without a trace. When ships sank, the ship and cargo were rarely recovered. Sometimes debris might wash ashore on Nantucket, furnishing salvage for beachcombers and scarce firewood for island homes. Over the centuries bits and pieces of vessels, origin unknown, have often drifted onto Nantucket's shores.

There was enormous loss of human life, as well. And so it was that the people of Nantucket, later supported by the Federal government, set about building the system of lights that would help warn of the dangers that surrounded their island home. Motivated both by humanitarianism and by canny business sense, the islanders created and maintained these lights both to beckon and to warn. "We're here," flickered the beacons of Brant Point, Sankaty Head,

The R.M.S. Olympic *glides by the Nantucket Lightship in heavy fog in April of 1934. A month later the lightship was rammed and sunk by the same liner.*

and Great Point. "Come in and welcome to ye, or pass by and Godspeed!"

The double message of Nantucket's lights underscores the ironies and contradictions of Nantucket's geographical situation. A beautiful summer day on this magnificent island makes it difficult to conceive of the ominous threat to navigation that the deep blue seas surrounding Nantucket can hold for the unsuspecting mariner. Hector St. John de Crève-coeur, standing on the shore of Nantucket facing the sea-borne wind, said it well:

Who can see the storms of wind, blowing some-times with an impetuosity sufficiently strong even to move the earth, without feeling himself affected by the sphere of common ideas? Can this wind which but a few days ago refreshed our American fields, and cooled us in the shade, be the same element which now and then so power-fully convulses the waters of the sea, dismasts vessels, causes so many shipwrecks, and such extensive desolation? How diminutive does man appear to himself when filled with these thoughts, and standing as I did on the verge of the ocean!

This is the story of Brant Point, Great Point, and Sankaty Head lighthouses and of the Nantucket South Shoals Lightship. It is also the story of those who manned them so heroically. Picturesque as they are, lighthouses and lightships deserve to be known as more than tourist attractions. The lights have an intrinsic value, but even greater is their spiritual value, a value reflected in the people, rarely acclaimed or even documented, who tended the lights. Day in, day out, the lights of Nantucket saved lives and spoke as the island's voice amid the sea that surrounded and dominated it.

Nantucket, more than many places, inspires our love through both its natural beauty and its rich history. Preservation of this history involves much more than nostalgia and its appeal to the eye of the tourist; it involves making a commitment to understand the sweep of history and the lives of those who made it. *Nantucket Lights* was written to remind us of the need to achieve that understanding, in the belief that the time is ripe to preserve that part of Nantucket's history that is represented by these illustrious beacons.

Those of us who experience Nantucket today value every grain of her sand, every drop of water in her seas, and every particle of salt in the air we breathe. We hope that this book will help the reader share that feeling, and we hope as well to bring forth something of the heart and spirit that have illuminat-ed the Nantucket lights. Having lost much of their practical value as navigational tools, these guardians now stand as monuments to the unsung heroes and heroines who kept them and to the quiet, committed service they gave to humanity. Perhaps we can now do our part to protect Nantucket's lights, as they have protected us and those who have gone before us.

Chapter One

GOD MADE THE WORLD
AND NANTUCKET

*On the seashore at Nantucket, I saw the play of the Atlantic with the coast. Here
was wealth; every wave reached a quarter of a mile along shore as it broke....
Ah, what freedom and grace and beauty with all this might!...Place of winds,
bleak, shelterless, and when it blows, a large part of the island is suspended in the
air and comes into your face and eyes as if it was glad to see you.*

--Ralph Waldo Emerson (1847)

Thirty miles off the Massachusetts coast lies Nantucket, a sandy intermediary between the rocky body of
New England and the open and often formidable Atlantic. Geologically speaking, Nantucket is a left-
over, the remnant of a world now lost beneath the waves that surround it. Some seventy million years
ago a vast lowland plain, made up of eroded material washed down from towering mountain ranges, stretched up
and down the Atlantic seaboard. This plain, broken by low hills separated by flat, valley-like depressions, ran north
and south, generally parallel with what is North America's present shoreline. As the ocean's waters rose, they submerged most of the plain; Nantucket Island, a mass of debris piled up by the last glaciers of the Ice Age, is one of
the few remaining hilltops visible above the ocean.

The contours beneath the shallow waters of Nantucket Sound, separating the island from Cape Cod, are also
part of this once vast coastal plain. Mariners entering these waters from the east between Great Point on Nantucket and Monomoy Island just off (and sometimes attached to) Cape Cod or from the west through Vineyard
Sound must plot a course through shoal-ridden waters with notorious currents and tidal rips. Although few of
America's waterways are as well traveled as these, they can still baffle even the most sophisticated navigational

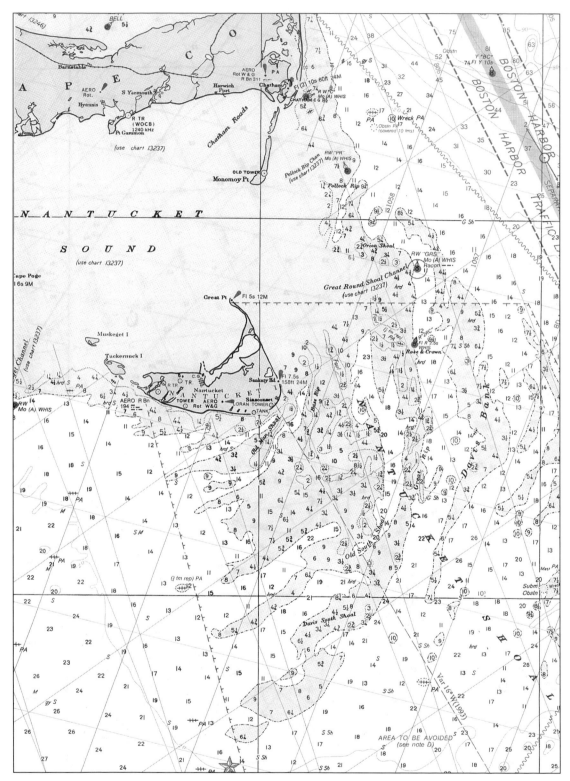

Chart of the shoals lying to the eastward of Nantucket. "Davis South Shoal" determined the placement of Sankaty Head Lighthouse as well as the position of the Nantucket Lightship.

system, as the crew of the *QE2* discovered to its chagrin when their ship ran aground in Buzzard's Bay to the west of Nantucket in the summer of 1994.

The outer, or southern, edge of this pile of glacial debris, known as a terminal moraine, reaches Nantucket from a westerly direction as it cuts across Tuckernuck Island. Farther east it forms a ridge going west to east across Nantucket itself. From there it drops below the sea's surface, creating the dangerous Nantucket Shoals that lie to the south-southeast of the island. The *Atlantic Coast Pilot* described Nantucket Shoals as "one of the most dangerous parts of the coast of the United States for the navigator." The shoals corrugate wide areas of the sea floor, and in some spots gargantuan boulders, bull-dozed down from the north by the glacier, lie menacingly on the ocean's bottom. The tops of the shoals are only three or four feet beneath the water's surface in places, with heavy breakers crashing over them. With frequent high winds, fast-running tides, and unpredictable wave formations created by powerful tidal flows, the shoals have swallowed whole more than their share of ships that have ventured too close. Other cases followed an equally tragic pattern: rudder damage—helpless drifting—grounding within sight of Nantucket's shore.

This dangerous underwater web entices mariners in several ways. As luck would have it, the Nantucket Shoals lie squarely in the path of the most direct shipping route between the ports of the northeastern United States and Europe. There is also the attraction of rich fishing grounds on the shoals and on Georges Bank, ninety miles to the east. Like moths to a flame, sailors eager to find the shortest route to New York or the quickest place to fill their ships' holds with fresh fish are drawn to these waters in large numbers.

Nantucket Shoals played a role in America's early history. The Pilgrims made their first landfall in the New World at what is today Provincetown at the end of Cape Cod, but their intended destination was the Hudson River in what is now New York. Even though many were sick and dying, the Pilgrims set sail from Cape Cod in a southerly direction, eager to complete their journey, but encountered the treacherous shoals just off Nantucket. Exhausted, fearful of shipwreck, and mindful of the season—late autumn—they chose not to tempt fate and turned back. Plymouth, on the shores of Massachusetts Bay, became their new home.

Bathed by the Gulf Stream, Nantucket has a more moderate climate than New England's mainland. North of Nantucket winters are more brutal, summers hotter. The island's climate is such that it can generally be reached by water year round with only minor interference from the weather. Occasionally the harbor freezes solid for as long as a week, but that is rare. At the same time, though, the warm waters of the Gulf Stream generate the great fog banks that hang almost continuously off the island. A

An aerial shot of Great Point Lighthouse in 1985 following a powerful storm. Note the break at The Galls that has made the Point an island, although currents soon shifted enough sand to fill the gap and restore Great Point to Nantucket.

fog bank needs only a little prodding from the breeze to enshroud the "Grey Lady"—an additional threat to the safety of those who ply Nantucket waters.

All told, Nantucket's natural advantages and scenic beauty are very nearly offset by the island's natural hazards. As Crèvecoeur noted, Nantucket "appears to be the summit of some huge sandy mountain, affording some acres of dry land for the habitation of man; other submarine ones lie to the southward of this, at different depths and different distances. This dangerous region is well known to the mariners by the name of Nantucket Shoals." Paradoxically, these mountains of sand are also "the bulwarks which so powerfully defend this island from the impulse of the mighty ocean, and repel the force of the waves; which, but for the accumulated barriers, would ere now have dissolved its foundations, and torn it to pieces." Nantucket's very existence represents a bargain between the benevolent forces of geological history and the less kindly caprices of weather

The steamship Nobska *sails through a narrow channel in the ice of a frozen Nantucket Harbor during World War II. Brant Point Lighthouse guards the harbor entrance.*

In 1917 the harbor froze; here the Coast Guard vessel Acushnet *makes its way through the ice past a crowd of curious citizens.*

and tide—although the great Northeasters of recent years seem to have speeded up the weathering of the island's shoreline, much to the dismay of property owners in some of Nantucket's beachfront enclaves.

Although Nantucket Shoals and Georges Bank absorb some of the force of the brutal ocean storms, time and tide bring about never-ending change. As Ralph Waldo Emerson said of Nantucket, "They say

here that a northeaster never dies in debt to a south-wester, but pays all back with interest."

A Northeaster (or No'theaster or Nor'easter, as these storms are familiarly known at various points along the New England coast), a type of storm indigenous to Nantucket and New England, occurs when a mass of cool, high-pressure air moving down from Canada encounters warm, moisture-laden, low-pressure air coming up along the coast from the south. The resulting high-energy but unstable storm system, rotating counterclockwise, draws cold, stinging winds and rain or snow directly off the cold waters of the North Atlantic and onto the shore with predictably unpleasant, and sometimes dire, results.

For all the damage they do on shore, Northeasters are also responsible for dramatic changes in the underwater terrain of shoal areas. Shifts in the sandy bottom topography brought about by violent storms on Nantucket Shoals have led many an experienced ship's captain to a mortal encounter with previously uncharted shallows.

The tides on Nantucket, on average, are much less than the ten-foot tides on the bay side of Cape Cod. Small though they are, they are not to be taken lightly. In 1869 the United States Coast and Geodetic Survey, reporting on the strong tidal currents around Nantucket, said: "There is no other part of the world, perhaps, where tides of such very small rise and fall are accompanied by such strong currents running far out to sea." A rip is an area within the shoal where

Swirls in the sand formed by currents of water and wind at Great Point in the 1930s.

tides may move especially fast or produce unpredictable cross currents. Numerous rips, some historically notorious and others less well known but equally treacherous, dot the seas around Nantucket, ready to wreck the unwary or the unlucky.

Nantucket's waters are an active, vibrant, moving system of forces that have no regard for man's wishes. The tides, winds, and weather will push and pull, molding Nantucket and the surrounding sea bottom to their own design.

By virtue of those forces and her geological location, Nantucket Island, for all her seductive beauty, has seen more than its share of the drama and tragedy of shipwreck. The island's mariners, forced by the economic necessity of their locale to challenge nature on a regular basis, have over the centuries journeyed far out into ocean waters, but one lesson they learned time and again was that their home waters were little safer than mid-ocean.

It was inevitable that Nantucketers, a logical and methodical people, would turn their energies toward developing a systematic approach to making this nautical environment safer. Beginning over 250 years ago, the islanders built and maintained a system of beacons to aid and guide mariners. By the end of the eighteenth century, those lighthouses and the men operating them had become part of an extensive and secure national system of navigational aids.

Each of Nantucket's legendary beacons was built with special characteristics to provide safer passage for the mariner. To guide sailors far out at sea from Sankaty Head and Great Point, tall lighthouses of classical design were erected. Their slim towers were tapered to keep them stable in high winds without additional structural support. Brant Point, as a harbor light warning of the Nantucket Bar close by, did not need height; today it still greets those who come to the island by sea with its distinctively squat and benevolent profile. The Nantucket South Shoals Lightship, anchored adjacent to the shoals with lights aloft on forty-foot masts, warned of immediate danger in the sometimes fierce Atlantic. Each of these lights played its part in protecting those who would venture near the island, and the tale of each is a distinct chapter in Nantucket's maritime and cultural history.

Chapter Two

THE WHALER'S LIGHT WITH NINE LIVES

BRANT POINT LIGHTHOUSE

Nantucket itself is a very striking and peculiar portion of the National interest.
There is a population of eight or nine thousand persons, living here in the sea,
adding largely every year to the National wealth by the boldest and most
persevering industry.

--Daniel Webster (1828)

Established before this country was born, Brant Point Lighthouse has welcomed countless Nantucketers home from the sea. The light survived the American Revolution, witnessed the greatest age of Nantucket whaling, and later watched whaling's demise. Brant Point then bade "farewell" to many Nantucketers lured away by the Gold Rush just after a third of the town was consumed by fire. Decades later, Brant Point light saw mainlanders come to summer on Nantucket. Islanders, summer people, and tourists alike thrill to the sight of this smallest of lights on their approach to Nantucket Island. When departing, the same people superstitiously throw their pennies overboard as they pass Brant Point Lighthouse. Few among us would not dare to do so, bidding farewell to this "good luck light" and ensuring that we will again some day be "coming 'round Brant Point."

Brant Point Lighthouse has always been a sentimental favorite of Nantucketers and tourists alike. More than a good luck charm, it is also an apt background for a photograph of a blushing bride on her wedding day or a pleasant spot to watch the endless boat traffic entering and leaving Nantucket harbor. Once seen, the picture-book quality of Brant Point Lighthouse is never to be forgotten.

Brant Point Lighthouse sits guarding the entrance to Nantucket harbor from a sandy point where Brant

The side-wheeler Nantucket, *her paddle wheels engine churning, rounds Brant Point. The* Nantucket *was in service from 1886 until 1913.*

geese were once so abundant the area was named for them. The light has had a turbulent history, having been built first in 1746 and subsequently rebuilt eight times—in 1758, 1774, 1784, 1786, 1788, 1825, 1856, and finally in 1901.

Home to a thriving native community in the mid-seventeenth century, Nantucket's relative isolation soon attracted English settlers from the Massachusetts Bay Colony. Seeking refuge from the religious rigidity of the Puritan establishment on the mainland, the early colonists first planned to farm and graze sheep on this sandy bit of land. Like their Indian neighbors, they too learned that nautical pursuits were more fruitful.

Fishing was an important part of the settlers'

livelihood from the first, but soon enough a new source of income and resources became apparent: right whales, whose migrations brought them close along Nantucket shores in the winter. The Indians taught the settlers what they knew about hunting the whale, and the colonists soon developed considerable skill. Combining this with entrepreneurial talents they brought from England, the newly arrived Nantucketers rapidly developed an industry based on the capture and processing of the whale.

Whaling proved extremely profitable from the start. Quite quickly Nantucketers became renowned for their whaling expertise, and soon virtually all business generated on the island was related to whaling. In colonial times whale oil was a valuable commodity, even more so than modern-day petroleum. An excellent source of illumination and a superb lubricant, the fruit of the whalers' harvest was in great demand, and as a result Nantucketers prospered.

In 1712 the first sperm whale was taken by a Nantucket whaler out in "the Deep," as distinguished from along the shore. Producing a high-quality oil, the sperm was obviously worth traveling any distance to capture, and so Nantucket's whale fishery began its development into a global enterprise. In the next century and a half, adventuresome Nantucketers would make of the sea an intricate network of well-traveled waterways leading around the world from their island home.

A few miles west of what is today Nantucket Town, early settlers had built the village of Sherburne on the rather small and shallow Capamet Harbor at Capaum. Within three generations, tumultuous storms had washed large quantities of sand into the mouth of the harbor, rendering it useless. By 1722 the town had moved to its present location on the more suitable Great Harbor, today called Nantucket Harbor. This body of water was deep and well protected, ideal for the whaling ships so vital to the townspeople's livelihood. In 1795 the relocated settlement took the name of the island—Nantucket, an Algonquin word meaning "land far out to sea." With the expansion of the whaling industry, the island's population increased, and so did its need to accommodate growing commerce. To allow cargoes to be landed directly on shore, Straight Wharf was built in 1723, permanent and tangible evidence that the little village was on its way to becoming a thriving seaport whose people would be renowned as seafarers.

The negative was that the sea was not always a kindly master. The wrecking of vessels, loss of valuable cargo and the drowning of entire crews was an all too common occurrence. The joys of prosperity were clouded by those tragedies. Coastal trade, of necessity a year-round venture, was carried on in largely uncharted waters and subject to severe New England weather. As whalers pressed on into "the Deep," it was sometimes their own home waters that proved most perilous. There arose a pressing need for ways to increase the safety of mariners and their ships.

At the mercy of winds and tides, a ship might approach Nantucket at any hour. Early on, lanterns burning in windows at night and local knowledge were the sailor's only guides through the dark channel into the harbor of Nantucket (then Sherburne) Town. The arriving mariner had to be alert to nuances of wind and current as well as to the dangerous Nantucket Bar, a long shoal extending two miles off the north shore of the island from Madaket all the way to Great Point. Directed only by the wind and his own skill, a ship's master had to rely on the most subtle of clues to reach safe harbor. As commerce increased, it was obvious that more than lanterns burning in windows would soon be needed to guide ships safely into the Port of Nantucket.

FIRST BRANT POINT LIGHTHOUSE—1746

The mariners of Nantucket had seen the Boston lighthouse, built in 1716 and the first to be established in the young colonies. Some had also seen lighthouses on their voyages to Europe. Early on they had realized that a lighthouse would help guide their vessels into the Great Harbor of the town and also warn mariners of the Nantucket Bar that both menaced approaching ships and blocked the passage of large or heavily laden ships. The Bar was a serious impediment to Nantucket's commerce. Obed Macy, in his 1835 *History of Nantucket*, describes the problem:

> *The harbor was protected by two points of beach, about three quarters of a mile apart, one on the east called Coatue, the other on the west side, called Brant Point. Nearly two miles from shore, to the northward of the harbor, is a bar, which all vessels, coming in and out, are under the necessity of passing. Vessels drawing nine feet of water may, with good pilots, pass over this bar and into the harbor. When a vessel comes to the bar drawing too great a draft of water to admit of her passing it with safety, lighters are sent, into which her cargo is discharged til she is sufficiently lightened.*

The whaling merchants and sea captains of the island soon urged that a lighthouse be built on Brant Point at the entrance to the harbor, and so in 1746 the Town of Sherburne erected what was then only the second lighthouse in the colonies. The first, Boston Light, was built on Great Brewster Island in 1716 and later moved to its current location on Little Brewster. This makes Brant Point the oldest lighthouse site in continuous use in the United States (see sidebar).

The records make it very clear that the town expected shipowners to repair and keep the light burning themselves, even though it was constructed on town property. The original lighthouse undoubtedly was not very sturdy, for it was haphazardly built, being designed as it was constructed. Wood was scarce on the island, but Nantucketers were adept at improvising and making do with what was on hand. Nonetheless, the very existence of the Brant Point light, despite its primitive structure, is indicative of Nantucket's prominence as a seaport at that early period. The first Brant Point Lighthouse was destroyed in 1757 by a fire, no doubt started by the crude whale-oil lamps used at that time. Those early lighthouse lamps left much to be desired, having a wick (hence the nickname "wickies" for lighthouse keepers) fitted into a spout connected to an oil reservoir but without a glass chimney. Oil could easily overflow from the spout of the smoky lamps, carrying flames downward into the pans designed to catch the surplus oil. Fire was a common occurrence at lighthouses, and Brant Point was no exception.

the General Court and request that 'Light Money' may be paid by all the shipping using this Harbor....

The last provision was the thrifty island way of enlisting the power of the colonial government to establish the right to the collection of fees to defray the enormous cost of rebuilding and maintaining Brant Point Lighthouse.

Since many captains from other ports objected to the lighthouse dues, the town was compelled to validate its tax. It petitioned the General Court (the legislative body) of Massachusetts for permission to levy tonnage dues, and on June 17, 1774, the Court authorized a "Light Money" tax to be levied on shipping. The proceeds would be given to the selectmen of the Town of Sherburne to control and maintain the light, thus keeping control of Brant Point Lighthouse in the hands of local authorities. In granting the

THE OLDEST LIGHTHOUSE?

For years a controversy existed as to whether Brant Point might be the oldest lighthouse in the United States. Nantucket pride played no small part in this dispute, as this letter demonstrates:

New Haven, Conn., Feb. 18, 1885

I am so tenacious in regard to the fame of dear old Nantucket, that it is with reluctance I pen that which truth and historic accuracy demand that I now write, viz.: That I must stop saying that Nantucket has the honor of having erected the first lighthouse.

In Godfrey's "Nantucket Guide" it is stated that on Brant Point "was erected the first beacon for vessels ever built in the United States. This occurred in 1746." In a parenthesis, we are told, on the same page (p. 216) that "the lighthouse on Little Brewster island, north side of main outer entrance to Boston Harbor, was established in 1754." All this I have long believed, and have never refrained from singing the praises of my Nantucket ancestors who thus wisely and kindly care for the mariner, and bade the lighthouse fire blaze

"Like a star in the midst of the ocean."

About two years ago the private secretary of our lamented fellow-Nantucketer by birth and descent, Hon. Charles J. Folger [U.S. Secretary of the Treasury from 1881 to 1884], *ventured to differ with me as to the claim which he learned I had made in behalf of Nantucket, and now my triumphant, though courteous, opponent, has forwarded to me the Annual Report of the Lighthouse Board for 1884, and in it, on the 10th page, indicated to my eye by a red pencil-mark, are these words, which I ruefully read and reluctantly accepted as an overthrow of my claim: "There was presented to the Board by Lieut. C.H. West, U.S.N., now on lighthouse duty, an old framed mezzotint engraving, made in 1729 by William Burgis, of the first lighthouse built on this continent. It was erected on Little*

continued on page 17

An echo of days gone by, the topsail schooner Shenandoah *ghosts out of Nantucket Harbor, fueling the imagination of an admiring audience.*

town's request, the Court proclaimed:

> *Whereas, the Inhabitants of the Island of Nan-*
> *tucket, at their own cost and charge, have at dif-*
> *ferent times erected Light houses upon Brant*
> *Point at the entrance of the harbor of Nan-*

> *tucket…the third (of which) is now standing,*
> *and is absolutely necessary for all vessels coming*
> *in and going out of said harbor, but the inhabi-*
> *tants of said Island have hitherto been at the*
> *charge of erecting and maintaining the said*
> *Light house, which burthen ought in equity to be*

born by all vessels receiving advantage from that Light belonging to Strangers as well as the said Inhabitants who have petitioned this Court for Relief.

Thus, each vessel over fifteen tons that entered or left Nantucket Harbor after August 1, 1774, was subject to a charge of six shillings, to be paid no more than once a year.

By the spring of 1775, war between England and the colonies had become a reality. The whaling fleet returned to Nantucket, bringing the industry to a near standstill for most of the Revolutionary War. As most were Quakers, Nantucket's citizens proclaimed neutrality, angering both sides of the conflict. As an isolated and vulnerable island community, Nantucket desperately needed either to find the shield of a well-armed protector or to maintain the appearance of complete innocence in order to protect itself.

In the end, Nantucket achieved neither. The town actu-

Brewster island, in Boston Harbor, in 1715-16, at the cost of £2,385, 17s, 8 1/2d, at the expense of the general court of the Province of Massachusetts Bay. It was maintained by the exaction of one penny per ton on all in-coming and out-going vessels except coasters, and these light-dues were levied by the collector of imports at Boston. This rare print shows an armed British customs pinnace at anchor near the light, and as it is interesting for its representation of the first lighthouse in this country, it is reproduced in this report." The engraving faces the title page and represents a tall, white lighthouse, with low, two-story house attached, the whole appearing very much like ours at Great Point. I yield the point as gracefully as can be expected, considering that I very much prefer to have Nantucket at the head of the class as often as possible.

Yours for truth at all hazards,

Phebe A. Hanaford

Phebe Hanaford, a 'Sconset-born Universalist minister, teacher, and suffragist, was well known as the author of several important biographies, including *Women of the Century* and a popular life of Lincoln.

Brant Point's claim to primacy also needed to be defended against supporters of Beavertail Lighthouse, located on Conanicut Island at the western entrance to Narragansett Bay. At least one formal quarrel, waged in the form of letters to the editor of a newspaper and documented in an 1880 scrapbook in the Nantucket Historical Association's collection, again displays the passion of Brant Point's partisans.

The first entry, dated August 14, 1880, states simply that Beavertail Light is the oldest on the coast, also mentioning Brant Point as "one of the oldest." The next entry is this article, signed "Islander":

In a recent letter to your paper from Nantucket I took occasion to correct a statement of a writer over the signature of F.D., which he had previously made in an article to a Providence

continued on page 19

ally petitioned the British, asking permission to continue whaling without the risk of capture, for the soil was not fertile enough to support the population by farming. Simultaneously, the town requested that the General Court of Massachusetts recognize the need for neutral status: "[T]he whaling industry cannot be preserved in this place....[T]he only possible remedy is in placing the island and its inhabitants in a state of neutrality." Neutrality was granted, but not respected.

Nantucket's wartime vulnerability was increased with the publication in England in 1776 of a chart that depicted the light at Brant Point and included the following sailing instructions: "To sail into Nantucket Harbor, and carry the best water over the bar on which [there] is 9 feet, bring the Lighthouse to bear S.S.E. then run for it, giving Brant Point a berth and Haul in. The Buoy on the East Flat is seen in day time."

It is safe to surmise that the light at Brant Point was periodically left unlighted during the war as a defensive measure, but trouble came nonetheless. Typical of Nantucket's wartime woes was an event on a night in September of 1781 when about a hundred well-armed Loyalist privateers came into Nantucket harbor and captured a few ships. The townspeople were afraid they would also come ashore, as had happened before. A message was sent to a small band of American forces on Cape Cod, who came to Nantucket later that night, exchanging shots with the privateers. The Americans placed several small cannons at Brant Point and the next morning opened fire and

sent the privateers hurriedly out of the harbor. Three days later the renegades (as such Loyalist raiders were known) came back and looted several more ships, setting one on fire.

Officially neutral or not, Nantucket was vulnerable to the fortunes of war. The Continental Congress, for its part, was ineffective (and not terribly interested) in aiding the remote island. The Royal Navy, on the other hand, was fully intent on destroying any and all American commerce, and Nantucket was as American as anywhere in its eyes. By the time the war was over, fifteen Nantucket vessels had been lost at sea, 134 had been captured (with their crews, many of whom languished for the duration aboard British prison hulks), and much cargo had found its way into the hands of British *and* American privateers. By the war's end, the once flourishing economy of Nantucket was in shambles.

The Nantucketers' litany of distresses and discontents extended beyond the war's end. In 1783 the crowning blow came in the form of a fire, probably started once again by the lamps, that destroyed the Brant Point Lighthouse.

FOURTH AND FIFTH BRANT POINT LIGHTS—1784 AND 1786

The burned light on Brant Point was replaced the next year by a "beacon" of uncertain quality that remained in service for only two years. It, too, was destroyed and then replaced by a similar beacon in 1786. When it blew down in a storm, the need was apparent for a substantial structure that could be relied upon to survive Nantucket's rigors.

Sixth Brant Point Lighthouse—1788

When the light at Brant Point was rebuilt for the sixth time, in 1788, the Commonwealth of Massachusetts provided the money to build it. The dim light and smaller size of this new beacon made it extremely unpopular with mariners and Nantucketers alike, but it was to do its job—however inadequately—for nearly forty years.

In addition to efforts to enhance the flame with different types of fuels, new reflectors of various sorts were used in conjunction with the light. A parabolic mirror was placed behind the flame creating light beams of

paper relative to the "oldest lighthouse on our coast." In my said letter, I stated that the first and oldest lighthouse was on Brant Point at the entrance to Nantucket Harbor, giving the date of its erection 1746. I also gave the date of the erection of the Beaver Tail lighthouse as 1761.

From the Town Records of Nantucket, I quote the following: "adopted in Town Meeting, January 24, 1746, "Voted, that the town will build a light house upon Brant point. Voted, that 200 pounds [sterling] *be raised for the towns use. Voted, that Ebenezer Calef, Jabez Bunker and Obed Hussey be the men to take care to build the light house."*

Again at a town meeting held at Nantucket, April 28, 1746, it was voted, that, "whereas there is a lighthouse built at the charge of the town in supposition that the owners and others concerned in the shipping, will maintain a light wherein, the town doth give them liberty to maintain the said light as they shall think to be most for their conveniency during the pleasure of the town."

To this "F.D." replied that Brant Point Light, though established before 1749, could not be called a permanent light until it was *legally* established. He claimed that Beavertail was legally established in 1749, while Brant Point, though in existence, was not legally established until some time after that.

"Islander" came back with a statement that "F.D."'s argument was almost too foolish to answer, and he hoped that any fair-minded and intelligent reader could distinguish the facts in both cases and arrive at a proper conclusion. He says in closing, "Here I rest the case, well-knowing that the truth of the claim made will stand on its own merits. [Signed] 'Islander.'"

And thus, the historical dispute between Rev. Frederic Denison (F.D.) for Beavertail Lighthouse, and Joseph E.C. Farnham (Islander) for the Brant Point Lighthouse, ended—and we all know in whose favor.

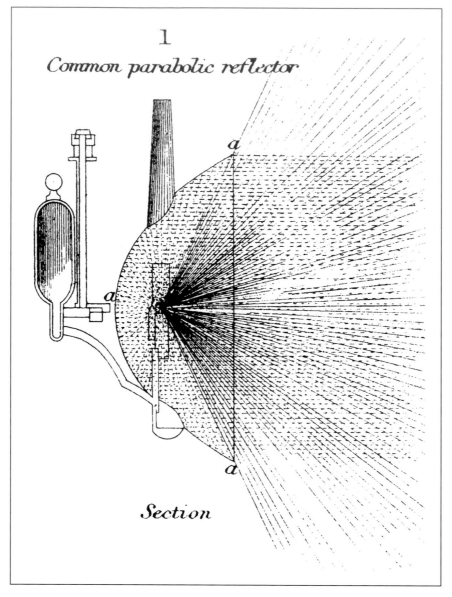

1

Common parabolic reflector

a

a

a

Section

Parabolic reflectors were among the advances in lighting that significantly improved the effectiveness of lighthouses in the eighteenth century. Such reflectors took advantage of new mathematical and optical principles that had been developed by Sir Isaac Newton and others.

to reduce the cost of keeping the lights burning. Lower-grade whale oil, more plentiful and half the price of sperm oil, became more generally used in the lighthouses. It did not burn as brightly as sperm oil, but an equal quantity would last twice as long.

Rebounding from wartime depression, Nantucket's whaling industry again flourished. In 1791 the first Nantucket vessels ventured into the Pacific in pursuit of whales, and their journeys were highly successful. The island prospered once again as the market for oil and candles grew.

By 1795 Brant Point Lighthouse, together with eight other lighthouses along the New England seacoast, was ceded to the federal government under the care of the first Secretary of the Treasury, Alexander Hamilton. The government was to take responsibility for protecting and fostering foreign trade, and putting coastal lighthouses under federal jurisdiction was the first of the new government's laws dealing with public works.

Although the War of 1812 once again devastated

equal intensity that could reach even farther toward the horizon from the light.

In the 1780s Brant Point was joined by an increasing number of lighthouses in Massachusetts, prompting the Secretary of the Treasury to seek ways

Nantucket's whaling industry, demand for its products quickly revived once peace was declared in 1815. Between 1820 and 1830, 237 whaling ships from the island were in service, typically setting out on voyages of three to four years into the Pacific Ocean in search of the diminishing stocks of sperm whales. During this, the "Golden Age of Whaling," Nantucket ships covered every ocean and sea on the globe, and Nantucket became a leading commercial center.

༄

Long a great hindrance to ships passing in and out of Nantucket harbor, the Bar across the harbor mouth became a more serious problem as whaling ships grew larger. These vessels, built for longer and longer voyages, were at first thirty- or forty-ton sloops. These gave way to brigs of fifty tons on average and later to even larger barks. As the whales became more scarce and planned voyages longer still, the ever-larger ships required a considerable depth of water. As cities like Boston illuminated their streets and the federal government built more lighthouses, pressure increased on the whale-oil industry to grow and become more efficient.

In an early bid to keep the port's competitive advantage, in 1803 Nantucket petitioned Congress to appropriate funds to dredge the channel from Brant Point to the outer part of the Bar and then to build stone breakwaters from Coatue and Brant Point to protect this channel. Congress rejected the petition, and so

the shallow entrance to Nantucket harbor threatened the viability of the island's whaling industry.

SEVENTH BRANT POINT LIGHTHOUSE—1825

By 1825 the lighthouse built in 1788 had deteriorated and was condemned. Congress appropriated $1600 for a new lighthouse to be built, along with an attached dwelling for the keeper and his family. The light itself was in a small tower framework built on top of the keeper's dwelling, and the mechanism consisted of eight lamps arranged in a double row, six in the lower series and two in the upper tier. To enhance the brilliance of the light, $12^1/_2$-inch reflectors were placed behind each of these lamps.

Obed Macy, the Nantucket Quaker historian and a scholar of strong opinions, offered this critique of the meagerly constructed 1825 lighthouse: "A strange constructed lighthouse is now erected on Brant Point. The keeper's house is removed about 50 rods to the eastward from its original location. On a 20 ft. roof above there is to be placed the lamps; which is to be supported by stout pieces of timber, with a head to cover the lamps. Instead of this there ought to be a high stone lighthouse placed at the end of the point."

Safe navigation in the harbor channel was becoming a growing concern, as Nantucketers realized that there were other seaports favorably situated and eager to compete for the whaling industry that

The Bug Lights in 1886. The Cliff area, just beginning to undergo development, is behind. The walkways made a sure all-weather path for the keeper of the lights.

Nantucket had created. In 1828 the islanders themselves arranged to dredge the channel, which almost immediately filled in again.

In lieu of improving the channel, the system by which it was marked had to be improved. In 1838 a pair of so-called "bug lights" were built below the Cliff area of Nantucket Town. These lights, when aligned with each other along the path of an approaching vessel, marked the route down the channel into the harbor. A keeper, Peleg Easton, was designated to tend the "bug lights."

During that same year Lieutenant Edward W. Carpender, U.S.N., made a rather unflattering report to the Lighthouse Establishment on his findings after visiting Brant Point Lighthouse:

Nantucket Harbor light…on the keeper's dwelling, on Brant point…consists of 8 lamps…. The upper lamps are entirely superfluous, and may with perfect propriety be suppressed. Indeed, I have reason to think that one-fourth the number of lamps, differently attended, would give more light; for, in the middle of the afternoon, (the keeper absent, to be gone until sundown, the hour of lighting) I found the lantern smoked, tube-glasses the same, lamps not trimmed, and reflectors really looking as if weeks or months had elapsed since they had been cleaned, they were so black and spotted.

The Lieutenant goes on to discuss the "Nantucket Beacon" at the end of Brant Point:

...placed as a range with the harbor light in guiding vessels across the bar. This beacon is a small building 11 feet high, in the window of which are two common lamps—one with three wicks, the other with two wicks. Very little attention has been paid to the neatness and cleanliness of this little establishment; the lantern in which the lamps are placed being exceedingly filthy, and one of the squares of glass, directly at the side of the light, out; some rags placed in its place with a stick. Two beacons, similar to this, are . . . at the head of Brant Point, opposite the best water on the bar, which will not, however, supersede the necessity for the present lights, the channel being intricate and narrow, and the depth of the water so small as to require the utmost aid from buoys and lights to vessels in picking their way into the harbor. . . There are four buoys and a buoy-boat on Nantucket bar, all of which are required by navigation.

The harbor channel was frequently shifting and silting up, forcing the use of an increasing number of beacons, buoys, and range lights in conjunction with the lighthouse. In 1839 a forty-two-acre parcel of land below the Cliff was sold to the United States as a site for the bug lights, known officially as "Harbor Lights." These were white range beacons, originally obelisks but later turret-shaped, placed 300 feet apart in the area near today's Jetties Beach to aid mariners passing over the Bar. The light farther from the beach had a fixed red light and the one closer to the beach had a fixed white light. The farther light was taller than the other, and when the mariner aligned the red light above the white one he knew he was entering the channel properly. After the jetties were begun in 1881, the bug lights became less necessary, and in 1908 they were discontinued and the land sold. (The Gilbreth house, of *Cheaper By the Dozen* fame, incorporates the last of the bug lights.)

In 1842 a floating dry-dock contraption known as "the camels" was devised to float ships over the Bar. A ship approaching or leaving the harbor would maneuver between the camels, and slings would be passed beneath the ship's hull. The added buoyancy of the camels would reduce the ship's draft, enabling it to clear the Bar. Although an elegant solution to the problem, the improvement was too little done too late. The value and profitability of Nantucket's whaling industry peaked that same year, and, although few realized it at the time, the industry itself was to be

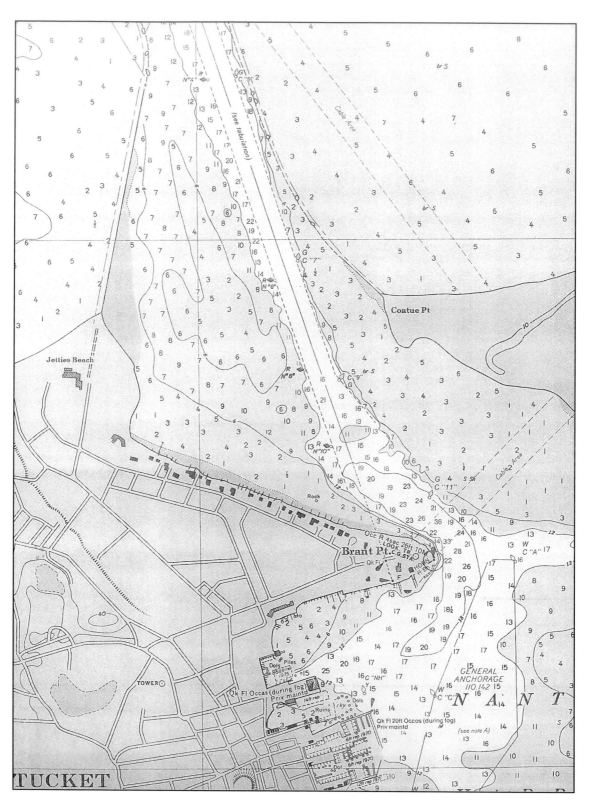

Portion of chart of the entrance to Nantucket Harbor, showing the extent of the jetties.

This later Bug Light was incorporated into "The Shoe," as Frank B. Gilbreth called his family's Brant Point cottage. This cottage would later be made famous in the book Cheaper by the Dozen.

short-lived. Soon enough the easy access to markets that the railroad gave New Bedford and then the discovery of petroleum in Pennsylvania would hasten the demise of Nantucket's whaling industry.

The Great Fire of 1846 destroyed the waterfront and over a third of Nantucket Town. Fortunately, Brant Point Lighthouse was spared. Big events were happening in the United States: coal gasification promised to improve illumination, the Gold Rush was about to begin, and the Industrial Revolution had taken hold in the young country. Much of the money earned by whaling went "'round Brant Point" in pur-

The Bug Lights looking east.

Out on Brant Point, looking northwest toward the west jetty.

suit of greater opportunities, with many of the Nantucketers themselves close behind. The island population declined from 9,712 in 1840 to 4,123 in 1870.

The flow of oil and money that the whaling industry brought to Nantucket marked the island's zenith as a maritime center. But the expanding global market for whale oil quickly grew beyond the carrying capacity of the sea and the sailors who hunted the sperm whale; cheaper, more accessible, and more plentiful substitutes were sought and found. Together, the effects of the 1846 fire, the Gold Rush, the railroad, the discovery of petroleum in Pennsylvania, and the Civil War were to bring the old whaling industry to a painful halt. In the broadest sense, modern technology had brought about its demise.

EIGHTH BRANT POINT LIGHTHOUSE—1856

Even with the whaling industry in its death throes and the population of the island declining, there was a demand in the 1850s for a more powerful light at Brant Point. Since the old lighthouse built in 1825 had "completely rotted," in 1856 the government authorized construction of a new brick lighthouse "with the least possible delay." It was "the wise policy of the [Lighthouse] board" to make all future construction permanent. Congress appropriated $15,000 to build a sturdy new lighthouse and keeper's house at Brant Point, about 135 feet south of the site of the earlier lighthouses. Today this structure is part of Brant Point Coast Guard Station.

First flight to Nantucket: On April 17, 1918 these two Navy "hydroplanes" drew a crowd to the Brant Point shoreline. Part of the Navy's anti-submarine effort during World War I, these Curtiss R-9s had flown in from the Naval Air Station at Chatham. Assigned to escort shipping in the area from the Nantucket South Shoals Lightship to Cape Ann, Georges Bank, and Gay Head, the R-9s were making something of a "courtesy call" on Nantucket. A total of four aircraft came to the island that day, including one that crashed while trying to land. Schoolchildren had been excused for the day to view what was for most their first glimpse of an airplane.

(Top) The 1856 Brant Point Lighthouse, early in its life. (Bottom) A later view of the 1856 lighthouse. The fence in the foreground may be a remnant of the one built in 1887 by the government to mark its claim on Brant Point; years of litigation ensued.

A permanent light tower was built. "The foundation of the tower is concrete," reports an official description,

> *two feet thick, and eighteen feet in diameter. The base is of hammered granite, laid in courses 2 feet thick to the height of 12 feet. The interior of the base forms a cistern, where water may be caught for household purposes. The column forming the tower is of brick laid in cement, with an airspace within the walls for ventilation. The lamp is of cast iron, with twelve lights of plate glass. A circular iron stairway winds its spiral way up to a floor of iron, where the lantern rests, 58 feet above the foundation and 47 feet above the ground. The lamp was a Catadioptric apparatus of the 4th order* [a reference to its size], *commonly called the Fresnel light.*

This light shone for the first time on December 10, 1856. In addition, the bug lights were refitted at that time.

❧

Jetties to protect the harbor entrance were finally started in 1881. The west jetty was built first, being completed in 1889; work continued, and the east jetty was finished in 1915. With the jetties to hold back the drifting sands, the channel was dredged, and access to the harbor of Nantucket became much easier for larger vessels. All of this was too late for the whaling industry; the last whaleship had sailed out of Nantucket harbor in 1869, never to return.

By narrowing the approach to the harbor, the jetties actually made it even more difficult to enter the harbor under sail. But the greater depth of the channel did accommodate the bulk of the steamers that brought passengers to the island in increasing numbers, although the need for various range beacons continued.

In 1887 a lengthy dispute began over the boundaries of the Brant Point Lighthouse site. In January of that year, the United States government notified surprised landowners on "the Point" that they were trespassing on government land. The Federal government proceeded to build a fence running through the properties of several residents and blocking the road to the Nantucket Hotel on Brant Point—already a flagship for the fledgling tourist industry. The government claimed that all land east of the fence had become theirs when Massachusetts ceded the Brant Point Lighthouse to the federal government in 1795. While the boundary dispute continued, permission was given to remove a portion of the fence during the summer season.

Failing to resolve the dispute by negotiation and unable to sue the federal government directly, the residents brought suit against the Brant Point lightkeeper, Joseph Remsen, and the fence builder as agents of the government. Depositions were taken and hearings were held. Highly esteemed lawyers representing both

The lanterns at the ends of the East Jetty had to be lighted by hand in the early days. This photograph, obviously taken in fine weather, gives little idea of what this task must have been like in winter or during a Northeaster.

sides of the case argued eloquently and vehemently over who owned the land in question. The dispute was finally resolved in 1901, when five lots, which had collectively made up the small piece of land that previously housed one of the old lights, were sold to three summer residents and the hotel. The government stated that the land was no longer needed for lighthouse purposes. The proceeds of the sale were paid to the U.S. Treasury.

As the whaling fleet vanished, a new industry was emerging on the island of Nantucket. Nantucket had been "discovered" as a summer resort. An increasing number of affluent people would journey to New Bedford and from there go on to Nantucket. "Summer people" arriving by steamship came down the channel into the heart of the island, where they found the quaint, quiet charm of a vintage seaport town, pristine beaches, and ocean waters ideal for bathing, sailing, and fishing. As residents of hotels and soon enough their own comfortable cottages, the summer folk found it easy to enjoy the placid splendors of Nantucket. The island in summer began to take on a look that combined its traditional Quaker modesty with a more forthright charm, and townspeople began to look forward to the town crier's shout of "Steamer's coming in! Steamer's rounding Brant Point!—two boats a day, now!"

Brant Point in 1956, showing the full length of the west jetty. The Coast Guard Station, with the tower of the 1856 lighthouse and the re-modeled Coskata Life Saving Station, is clearly visible.

Looking down Easton Street toward Brant Point in the 1890s. The steamship Island Home *passes the lighthouse, which had been painted white in 1885. The Nantucket Hotel dominates the Point to the left. Part of the hotel had formerly been a Quaker meetinghouse; later a section of it was moved across the harbor by barge to become the Dreamland Theater.*

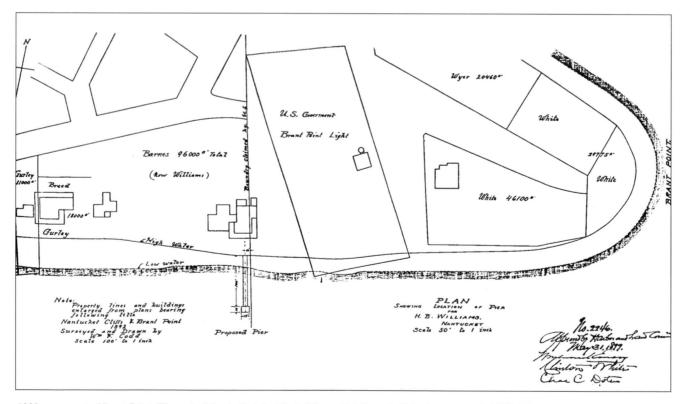

1899 survey map of Brant Point. The vertical line to the left of the lighthouse plot shows the Federal government's 1887 claim.

Easton Street attracts cyclists at the turn of the century. The 1856 Brant Point Lighthouse stands in the background.

NINTH BRANT POINT LIGHTHOUSE—1901

The present Brant Point Lighthouse was built in 1901 at the easternmost extremity of the point, 596 feet to the east of the 1856 brick lighthouse. It had become imperative to build a new, more easterly lighthouse on Brant Point, as the dredged channel was no longer aligned properly with the earlier light due to shifting caused by the jetties.

The new light's white cylindrical tower, twenty-six feet in height, is the shortest lighthouse on Nantucket—and in all of New England, for that matter. It is the least powerful of the three lights on the island, with an occulting red light of only 600 candlepower.

The tower originally housed a white light, the lantern taken from the 1856 light. It was changed to red in 1933 because, as the island became more settled, sailors complained that they confused the white light with the house lights dotting the island. Furthermore, vessels entering the harbor leave the red light to starboard, as is proper for navigational aids marking channels; the light atop the east jetty (passed to port on entry) is green.

In 1908, the changed course of the dredged channel also necessitated the installation of new range

(Top) Before: The 1856 lighthouse and the keeper's residence, sometime shortly before the construction of the "new" light in 1901. Monomoy, in the distance, is still undeveloped. The top section of this light, including the actual light mechanism, was moved to become the top of the 1901 tower. (Bottom) After: The 1856 lantern sits atop the new tower, although the railing around the older tower's top level remains in place at the time this photograph was made.

lights of skeletal construction housing fixed white lights. The old bug lights, in service since 1838, were then discontinued.

Brant Point Light is officially designated No. 15205 on the Coast Guard's current "Light List" of aids to navigation on the Atlantic coast. The mariner learns from the list that every four seconds Brant Point's light, sitting atop a white cylindrical tower, shines bright red in the dark of night or fog of day, visible for ten miles. The light is termed single-occulting, meaning the duration of light in a particular time frame is longer than the total duration of darkness. The intervals of darkness, called eclipses, are repeated on a regular basis. If the lighthouse light is displayed during the day (almost always because of fog) the horn also bellows its haunting note for one second out of every ten. By day, Brant Point's petite height and the wooden footbridge leading to the green door of the lighthouse are distinctive landmarks.

The last lighthouse keeper to man Brant Point was Gerald M. Reed, who arrived at his station on Brant Point in 1927 after serving, as had his father before him, at various lighthouses in New England. Members of his family still reside on Nantucket. Although the U.S. Coast Guard took over responsibility for operating the Brant Point Lighthouse from the

An early view of the 1901 Brant Point Lighthouse. The pilings, exposed to ice and water erosion at the time this photograph was made, were surrounded by piles of protective stone "rip-rap" in 1924.

An early image of the 1901 Brant Point Lighthouse, with the "topless" tower of the 1856 light clearly visible in the background.

U.S. Lighthouse Service in 1939, men like Gerald Reed never joined the Coast Guard. Fearful of change and of transfer from their beloved Nantucket, he and others like him served out their days as members of the Lighthouse Service to which they had long been dedicated.

In 1969 the Coast Guard initiated an aggressive program to automate the lighthouses. They were prompted by rapid advancements in technology and by the government's desire to be cost efficient. The days of lighthouses manned by dedicated keepers had become only a memory.

Today the Coast Guard Station at Brant Point

cares for both the existing Brant Point lighthouses, having its office and radio room in the 1856 structure, its red brick now painted a sparkling white, and operating the working 1901 light. Practically, the current light's function as a navigational aid is helpful but not essential, but romantically and aesthetically Brant Point Lighthouse remains as essential as it was in the days of the sailing ships of old.

On July 23, 1919, Mrs. Seth M. Ackley, whose husband was born on Nantucket and was a Rear Admiral in the United States Navy, summed up exquisitely the mystique, the romance and the cultist fervor of "coming 'round Brant Point" in her address to the

Twenty-fifth Annual Meeting of the Nantucket Historical Association:

> When I first saw the island in 1879 I sailed into the harbor on a government vessel, with my husband, then a Lieutenant in the Navy, who was detailed for Coast and Geodetic Survey work, which took us from Mexico to Maine. He was in command of the "Eagre", a yacht which had a tragic past, having been owned and sailed by Commodore Garner of the New York Yacht Club, and which, at anchor in New York harbor, was struck by a sudden squall, capsized and sank. Commodore Garner, his wife, and several guests were drowned. For some time the ill-fated craft found no purchaser but finally the government bought her and fitted her out for

The old Coskata Life Saving Station being floated past Brant Point Lighthouse in 1948 to become part of the Coast Guard Station at the Point. The structure in the foreground was known as the "Signal House." It housed the station's fog horn and bell. This photograph was taken from the World War II-era observation tower that still stood at that time.

Nantucket Harbor in the early 1900s. Two Brant Point Lighthouses can be seen.

Coast Survey work, and my first trip in her was from New York to Nantucket.

It was a different town through which we walked, after landing at the old wharf. There were no asphalted streets; all the shore from Brant point to the present bathing beach was over-grown with dusty-miller, goldenrod, aster, and lovely swamp honeysuckle, where now the fine summer cottages face the sea.

The Town Crier was going through the streets ringing his bell, and calling out "Sale of beef and mutton! Sale of beef and mutton down at Burgesses' market!" We passed a barrow, or stall in front of what is now Gardiner's Art Shop, where bluefish were exposed for sale, and beautiful they looked, gleaming silver in the evening light. I remember that they were 25 cents apiece. This sounds like a fable nowadays—a good fish story—but it is true.

I had never been in New England till that

Form 806
DEPARTMENT OF COMMERCE
LIGHTHOUSE SERVICE

JOURNAL OF LIGHT STATION AT *Nantucket Mass* —

19 41 MONTH	DAY	STATE WORK PERFORMED BY KEEPERS REGARDING UPKEEP OF STATION, AND RECORD OF IMPORTANT EVENTS, WEATHER CONDITIONS, ETC.
December	1	Routine
"	2	Routine Horn in Use
"	3	Horn in Use
"	4	Horn & Bell in Use
"	5	Horn & Bell in Use
"	6	Horn & Bell in Use
	7	Sunday Declared War Japan Dec 7, 1941
	8	Testing Horn
	9	Regular duties working on books. *Watching for Airplanes*
	10	Regular duties making signs for gates to elevator
	11	Regular duties
	12	Regular duties
	13	Regular duties
	14	Sunday
	15	Regular duties Asst away ½ day *leave absent*
	16	McDonald down to look over electric hand phone Jetty light extinguished low — gas in tank
	17	Relighted Jetty light put in 4 tanks
	18	Regular duties. Cleaning up about Sta.
	19	Polishing brass. Cleaning engine room
	20	Went out with C.G. to Extinguish Buoys
	21	Sunday.

The official journal of the Brant Point Light Station for December of 1941. Note Keeper Gerald M. Reed's notation regarding the attack on Pearl Harbor on the 7th; by December 9th, he was on the lookout for approaching aircraft.

day, and the little grey town, creeping up gentle inclines from the water's edge, struck me as having a very foreign air, so different in planned architecture from the places south of the Mason and Dixon's Line, to which I was accustomed. Everything neat, compact, meant to house people. I do not remember seeing a single veranda or porch, except the covered doorways, and my eyes were used to more verandah than house, both upstairs and down, for those wide galleries are the living rooms of Southern people.

If "Beauty is in the eyes of the beholder" mine were sadly lacking, for I saw no beauty, but was oppressed by the prim coldness of closed doors, the air of withdrawal and seclusion. Little did I think then that the time would come when I should write

> *In which of thy moods do I love thee best*
> *Dear Island of my choice?*
> *Basking in sun, veiled in thy mists,*
> *Or loud with the tempests' voice?*

Yet so it was, and, speaking of islands, we visited many, lived for three years in one, before the Long Trail ended, and in all of them found the distinguishing characteristic which marks the people of this dear spot—steadfast affection and loyalty to the birthplace. They wander far and near over the face of the earth, but wherever one meets them they are always planning "some day to go back home." Once as we were steaming into the harbor of Ceylon, a stalwart man standing on the landing stage, put his hand to his mouth, as we made fast, and shouted "Hello, Seth! Coming round Brant Point?"

What an evening they had! Coatue, the Haulover, Madaket, Sankaty, and Tuckernuck sounded strange enough in that island where the warm dusk was heavy with the odor of a thousand spices, amid palms and orchids, snakes and Cingalese. And that was only one of many ports where we saw familiar faces from the old home town, sailors mostly, for Nantucket has always pointed out to her sons the glittering treacherous highway, and they have followed it, many to the "vast and wandering grave," many to success and achievement in far countries.

We met a great old ruler of a small island, the Maharajah of Johore, who said "no one knows how beautiful an island can be until they have seen my island," and we did see it later on, and were his guests for an unforgettable fortnight, and surpassingly lovely it was after a wild, tropical, tangled fashion; but one night, after a day spent in watching the natives cut jungle (we were seated on elephants' backs to be out of the reach of venomous snakes, scorpions and leeches) my husband said "I would not exchange the whole of this poisonous island with all its Palaces, for standing room in Sauls Hills."

Two old views of steamship days at Brant Point: above, the inbound Gay Head *in 1912. Below, the* Sankaty, *the first propeller vessel built for the steamship line, in 1920. Watching ships "coming 'round Brant Point" has eternal appeal.*

The observation tower built at Brant Point to monitor harbor traffic during World War II dwarfs the lighthouse behind. A similar structure was built at Great Point.

So, and not otherwise, the hillman loves his hills; so, and not otherwise, Virginians love Virginia. Once in a small Virginia town a resident received a call from a new comer. After the guest had left, the little daughter of the house said to her mother, "Where did that lady come from?" The mother replied: "Hush, dear; you must never ask such a question; it would be embarrassing for her, for of course if she had been from Virginia she would have said so."

That is the way we feel about Nantucket. We say so. There may be the hoot of the motor horn in the once quiet streets, but sea and sky are unchanged, the moors still stretch crimson and purple, the pines point their lean green fingers away from the wind, and no matter where we wander, our hearts are always "coming 'round Brant Point."

Chapter Three

"AS GOOD A LIGHT
AS EVER WAS ANYWHERE"
GREAT POINT LIGHTHOUSE

Nantucket Island's Great Point, which reaches north toward Cape Cod's Monomoy, has a

glacial core; but its long hook is made of sand from the eastern headlands of Squam and

Sankaty. Thus, the currents which build onto Great Point flow northward toward the

entrance of Nantucket Sound. The presence of the Point itself has given rise to southward-

flowing currents which are widening Coskata Beach and building up Coatue Beach.

Coatue is a long bar, scalloped to perfection on the side facing Nantucket Harbor. Its

graceful pattern is the work of tidal currents which alternate up and down the coast, piling

sand first in one direction, then in the opposite.

--Barbara Blau Chamberlain,

These Fragile Outposts (1964)

Where Nantucket Sound meets the Atlantic, directly north of Great Point, lies the passage between Nantucket and the New England mainland, marking the eastward end of the "inshore" route along the southern New England coast. This route served the native peoples of New England for thousands of years before Europeans arrived, and for three centuries (before the opening of the Cape Cod Canal in 1914) it was the route of choice for coastal commerce. Connecting New York with New Haven, New London, Newport, Fall River, New Bedford, and then around the Cape to Boston and Down East, this corridor was America's turnpike, over which traveled fish, lumber, manufactured goods, farm products, and, of course (for a century),

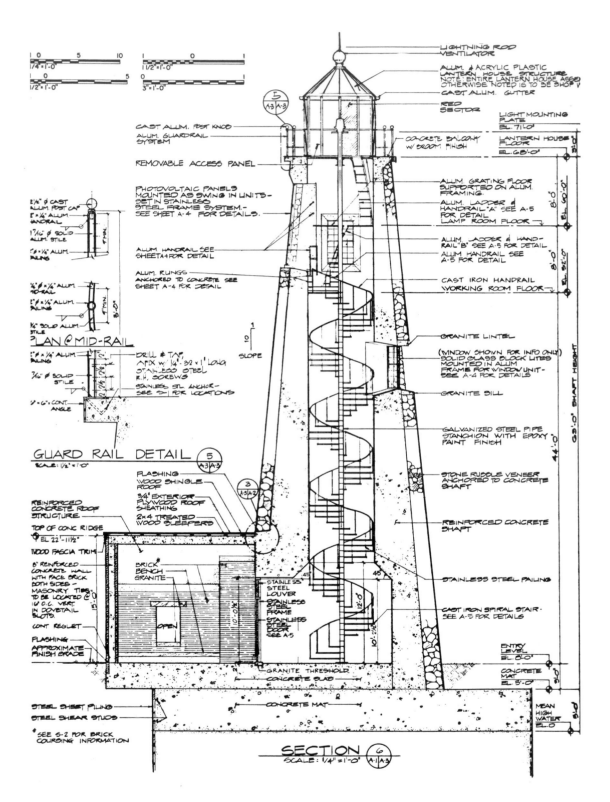

1985 plans for the reconstruction of the Great Point Light tower.

Spectacular photograph of Nantucket in the late 1800s, with the Horseshed still visible on Coatue across the harbor entrance.

whale oil. The efficiencies of sea transport, however, have always been to a degree offset by difficulty and danger. Heavy traffic, strong currents, shallow waters, and unpredictable weather play their part in making this route, in particular, a potential nightmare.

Nowhere was the danger greater than at the narrow point of passage between the inshore route and the open Atlantic. The tongues of sand that reach out to the north from Nantucket's Great Point and to the south from Monomoy on Cape Cod pose their own hazards, but the shallow and shoal-ridden waters to the east, with powerful tidal currents washing over them, are more treacherous still. The opposing cur-

rents and the shallows they wash—known as the Point Rip—that meet in this narrow passage make for the most actively changing waters off the Nantucket coast.

A lighthouse at Great Point, where the treacherous surrounding waters had caused many tragic maritime losses, was sorely needed to facilitate Nantucket's development as a seaport. It was imperative to reduce the dangers to vessels, cargo, and crew as they approached Nantucket.

In 1770 the Nantucket town fathers created a committee to ask the General Court of the Massachusetts Bay Colony to build a lighthouse at the end of Great Point, then called Sandy Point. The Nantuck-

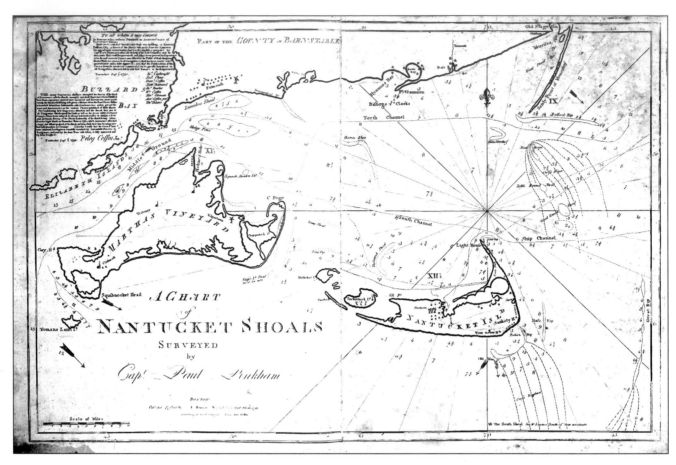

Great Point Lightkeeper Paul Pinkham's chart of the Nantucket Shoals, first published in 1790.

eters were impatient to have the light built, and to expedite their cause it was decided that they would send a local representative to Boston to "use his influence in the General Court to get a Light House on the Point according to his own discretion." At the time their efforts were fruitless; their proposal remained on the table but unresolved.

Despite the critical need for a light at Great Point, the issue languished through the Revolutionary War period. But on February 5, 1784, the Commonwealth of Massachusetts finally agreed to construct a

wooden frame lighthouse on "Sandy Point, Nantucket." Many early maps and charts and government light lists referred to this light as Nantucket Light.

The lighthouse was built very soon after the General Court approved its creation, completed in 1785 by Edward Allen and Stephen Hussey of Nantucket at a cost of 1,089 pounds, 15 shillings, and 5 pence.

The keeper of the new light had one of the most difficult stations in New England, for just in getting to his post he had to contend with Great Point's own natural hazards. The point is a barrier beach system, composed of glacial debris and soft sand. In winter the effects of wind, snow, waves, and ice would make the daily journey to and from the light a trial in its own right, although in more pleasant weather the trip, then as now, was achingly beautiful. For the first few years there was no housing for the keeper, who was expected to walk or ride his horse from Wauwinet to the light each day to light the lamp and then return home.

Fifty-year-old Captain Paul Pinkham, a man of considerable experience at sea, was the logical choice for the first keeper of newly constructed Great Point Lighthouse. Even with his extensive maritime knowledge, he received a conservative starting salary of $166.66 plus housing and twelve cords of wood, the latter a valuable commodity on Nantucket. Later, after many complaints, his salary was raised to $250 a year. The keeper had around-the-clock responsibilities whether calm or stormy weather conditions prevailed.

Along with manning the light, Captain Pinkham made a lasting and meaningful contribution to the lives of his fellow sea captains. Observing from the top of the lighthouse and drawing on his experience as a maritime pilot, Pinkham created the first accurate chart of the shoals around Great Point. In 1790 his chart was published by John Norman of Boston, selling at the prohibitive cost of $5.00. Pinkham's chart was highly praised by many shipmasters of the day as an invaluable aid in avoiding the hazards of the Point Rip.

Pinkham's life as keeper was rigorous. The only fresh water at his remote post was what he collected from depressions in the low dunes. For staples available only in town, Pinkham drove his horse and cart from the lighthouse to the western end of Coatue, where he had built a small shed to protect the horse from inclement weather. He then rowed across the Nantucket channel to Brant Point to get his "vittles." That route was six miles shorter than traveling through Wauwinet and around the island by land. A shoal off First Point on Coatue is still known as "the Horseshed" due to Lightkeeper Pinkham.

In August of 1789 Great Point Lighthouse, along with Brant Point and seven other lighthouses in Massachusetts, was placed under the jurisdiction of the new Federal government as part of the ninth law passed by the newly formed Congress:

AN ACT for the establishment and support of lighthouses, beacons, buoys and public piers.

BE IT ENACTED BY THE SENATE AND HOUSE OF REPRESENTATIVES OF THE UNITED STATES OF AMERICA IN CONGRESS ASSEMBLED,

That all expenses which shall accrue from and after the fifteenth day of August, one thousand seven hundred and eighty-nine, in the necessary support, maintenance, and repairs of all lighthouses, beacons, buoys, and public piers, erected, placed, or sunk, before the passing of this act, at the entrance of or within any bay, inlet, harbor or port of the United States, for rendering the navigation thereof easy and safe, shall be defrayed out of the Treasury of the United States.

Thus was born America's first provision for public works. This law put lighthouses under the direct supervision of Treasury Secretary Alexander Hamilton. The Secretary oversaw the lighthouse system personally until May 9, 1792, when he delegated the duty to the Collector of Customs. President George Washington, realizing the importance of maritime commerce as well as the pressing need for revenue from taxes levied on imported goods, also took a personal interest in the new nation's lighthouses.

Hamilton, in his first official report to President Washington on lighthouses, dated June 18, 1790, lists "Nantucket," referring to Great Point, as one of six lighthouses under his care in Massachusetts at that time. The report submits for approval Mr. Paul Pinkham to be the "officier" at the "Nantucket" lighthouse for the annual wage of $250; his counterpart at Boston was to receive $400. The Secretary's report also recommends to President Washington that the "distant" states (presumably those too far to supervise directly from the capital) follow a Massachusetts plan putting their lighthouses under the collectors of the principal ports, authorizing them to contract for maintaining the various lighthouses.

On December 16, 1795, Captain Pinkham wrote to the Superintendent of the Lighthouse Board seeking an increase in his salary and explaining why he felt he deserved it:

> *Sir:*
>
> *It is my ardent Request that you will be pleased to lay before the Honorable Senate and House of Representatives the enclosed, and make use of the utmost of your Influence to carry it into effect, as the Smallness of the Sallary renders it very hard for me to Subsist. The twelve cords of wood which was allowed me by the Legislature of this Commonwealth as part of my Sallary now costs $96 landed at the Lighthouse, provisions in like proportion & all other Necessaries of life. Therefore you must know that the Small Sum of $250 without any other natural advantages is a scanty support for a Family thus far removed from all other immoliments whatsoever. Now Sir your ernest attention to this shall be regarded and ever acknowledged by your humble Servant, Paul Pinkham*

Presumably, Pinkham's request was granted.

In an agreement between Keeper Pinkham and an assistant hired to aid him, glimpses of life at Great Point Lighthouse are revealed. For an annual wage of $180, the assistant is to "keep the lighthouse in good order, as well as attending to other duties, such as fetching oil, wood and hay and other necessaries, and not to neglect his duties." The assistant was also to receive "one-half of all Drifts and Prizes he shall obtain in the service and one half of all Shark Oil and fish he shall catch . . . [and] one-half the profits of the two cows said Pinkham shall keep, he paying one half the charge arising on said cows." For living quarters he was allowed to use "the east bed chamber, one-half the kitchen and milk room" of the lightkeeper's house.

On June 1, 1795, Nantucket's first bank, appropriately named the Nantucket Bank, opened for the first time. Three weeks later robbers broke into the bank, absconding with $20,000, all in heavy gold and silver coins. The three robbers, off-islanders whose identities were eventually revealed after years of rumor and recrimination on the island, had originally sailed to Nantucket on business and supposedly left for home. On the foggy night of the crime, instead of sailing off in their sloop they anchored just off Great Point. Stealing Keeper Pinkham's lighthouse rowing vessel, they returned to town, plundered the bank, and then made several trips through the gloom to load their booty before making their getaway. Keeper Pinkham had to write to his superiors telling of the loss of government property, for he was accountable for all property issued to him by the Lighthouse Administration. He also published this notice, which contains a rare and colorful description of the small vessels used at lighthouses in that period:

> *Nantucket, June 24, 1795*
>
> *Last night between ten o'clock and daylight next day was stolen from the lighthouse landing the*

Alexander Hamilton. As the first Secretary of the Treasury, Hamilton was given responsibility for developing the nation's lighthouse system.

> *light house boat, in length eighteen 1/2 feet, breadth about eight feet, with three sprit sails, a Road Anchor, and painted with a White Bottom, the top streak yellow and the next to that black; her inside painted Red; the mast yellow in the middle and Black at each end; a Black Stern and a White Strake around her stem—being the property of the United States. Whoever will Deteck the thief and return the property shall be handsomely Rewarded by Paul Pinkham, Keeper of the Lighthouse at Nantucket.*

Iron filigree of the spiral staircase in the 1818 Great Point Lighthouse tower. Note also the banks of batteries that powered the light in modern times.

Captain Pinkham died in 1799 at the age of sixty-four after helping to salvage the cargo of a schooner that had gone ashore on Great Point several weeks earlier. George Swain succeeded Captain Pinkham for a short time, followed by Jonathan Coffin, who once again was forced to make a daily trip to Great Point Lighthouse from his farmhouse after the lightkeeper's dwelling was destroyed by fire in 1812. Coffin's yearly salary was $196.67, including compensation for his lengthy commute.

In November of 1816, Great Point's wooden light tower was destroyed by fire. Although it was never proven one way or the other, there was strong evidence the fire was deliberately set. "It can hardly admit of a doubt . . . that the Lighthouse . . . was purposely set on fire," one observer noted at the time, although the nature of the evidence and the motive for such an act are unknown.

THE SECOND LIGHTHOUSE AT GREAT POINT—1818

Great Point Lighthouse was an important beacon, and its destruction prompted the federal government to move quickly to replace it. On March 3, 1817, the Fourteenth Congress of the United States appropriated $7500 dollars to rebuild it, and President James Madison signed the act into law. The lighthouse actually cost $7385.12 to construct.

By that time Brant Point Lighthouse had been destroyed and rebuilt more than any other light in New England, and Nantucketers were determined to make the new Great Point structure more permanent. Work began in the fall of 1817 on a durable sixty-foot lighthouse, and within two years masons had meticulously crafted a stately tower out of hefty blocks of cut granite. The tower encased a lace-like cast iron spiral staircase that gracefully wound its way to the top of the light. The lighthouse tower and the keeper's dwelling were connected by a short covered walkway to ensure that the keeper would have no difficulty getting to the tower to tend the light, even if snow were to drift heavily during the winter.

This lighthouse, which continued to be referred to on early charts as Nantucket Light, was considered, in the words of Nantucket historian Edouard Stackpole, "one of the best in the United States. The light, when kept in good order, shone more brilliant, it was said, than any other on the coast at that time. The

point, on which it stood, projected far out into the sea, which renders the light very beneficial to vessels passing through the sound." A Captain Smith described this light more succinctly in 1866 as being "as good a light as ever was anywhere."

This 1818 tower was painted white for visibility, and its fixed white 12,000 candlepower beam could be seen for eleven miles. The lantern itself, was eight and a quarter feet high and nine feet in diameter, with fourteen lamps, three with 15-inch and eleven with 16-inch reflectors. The lamps were arranged in two circles parallel to each other and to the horizon.

In 1829 many Nantucket citizens and ship owners petitioned the Lighthouse Establishment to remove a Captain Bunker from his position as keeper of Great Point Lighthouse. The petitioners and accompanying letters alleged that Bunker was a man of intemperate habits. After an investigation it was ruled that the charges were unfounded and that the petition and letters were part of a politically motivated effort to have Bunker ousted from the job so that George Swain could be reinstated as keeper at Great Point. Captain Bunker remained at his post.

On September 27, 1857, a new Fresnel lens, similar to the one that Sankaty Head Lighthouse helped to pioneer in the United States in 1850, shown brightly for the first time at Great Point. Augustin Fresnel had created seven orders, designating the size and power of his lenses. The "order" refers to the distance from the light source to the lens. The most powerful

Bob Caldwell oversees the installation of the 1857 Fresnel lens and light mechanism removed from the Great Point Lighthouse at the Nantucket Life Saving Museum in 1972.

light would be created by the first-order lens, being the largest; the smallest, used mostly in harbors, was the sixth-order lens. The new Great Point beacon had a third-order lens, one order stronger than the one installed at Brant Point in 1856. At the same time, the tower was lined with brick and its height raised to seventy feet above the sea, improving visibility to fourteen miles. Whale oil had fueled the previous lantern, but the new Fresnel system burned a combination of colza, which is lard oil, and kerosene. That light proved to be very durable, shining brightly from Great Point Lighthouse for 114 years until its replacement in 1971. The Nantucket Life Saving Museum now displays the 1857 lens.

Even with a more powerful new light to guide mariners, the waters off Great Point continued to take their toll; the stories of shipwrecks there abound. The example of the schooner *Conanchet* gives an idea of the perils of Nantucket Sound. On January 23 of 1857, a

Great Point Lighthouse in the 1950s. The retaining wall at the base of the tower has been exposed in this photograph.

winter noted for its brutal cold, the *Conanchet*, headed for New York with a cargo of fish, became entrapped in the ice in Nantucket Sound. Abandoning the vessel just before it capsized, the crew proceeded to crawl on hands and knees across the surface of the fractured ice, supporting themselves with planks torn from the ship. The temperature stood at eleven degrees above zero; it took them nine hours to safely reach shore at Great Point, where they were undoubtedly very happy to spend the night with Keeper Swain.

In 1861 the top of the tower and the old lantern were removed and replaced with a new iron deck and a new lantern of iron and copper. The Nantucket *Weekly Mirror* in a joking manner extolled the virtues of the improvements, writing that "The new light may be seen over four-fifths of the circle of the horizon, the one-fifth towards this place is the part which does not give the full light though visible. . . . The remaining one-fifth would be of no use to sea navigation. We say water navigation, because it may be of some use

The 1818 Great Point Lighthouse as it was in Lizzie Coggeshall's day. The covered walkway from the house to the tower is clearly visible.

sometimes to those who in the 'dry' season cannot see hardly how to navigate themselves."

The lightkeepers at the time kept count of vessels that passed their station, and it was not unusual for a thousand vessels to pass in a ten-day period. With the volume of ships came a comparable volume of shipwrecks. Between 1863 and 1890 the keeper's journal from Great Point records forty-three wrecks that occurred within the light's range. Because they looked similar from a distance, Great Point Lighthouse, Cross Rip Lightship, and Handkerchief Lightship were often confused with one another. Ship after ship would tell the same story of mistaking the light for one or the other of the lightships, then going aground on the Great Point Rip. This went on for years. The reports of the wrecks would be sent to the Lighthouse Board in Washington, but nothing was done to rectify the situation.

The degree of loss varied. Often the vessels themselves were lost, but usually the crews were saved. In the year 1804, for example, the schooner *Republican*, loaded with barrel staves, came ashore near the lighthouse. When the vessel struck the shoals, the ship's captain and his wife swam ashore. George Swain, the keeper, took good care of the couple, even purchasing the wreck for $50. The remnants of the vessel served him for firewood, wood having become so scarce on the island that Melville was to remark in *Moby Dick* that "pieces of wood in Nantucket are carried about like bits of the true cross in Rome."

Great Point was a very isolated station, and the isolation told on the families of the keepers. At the age of nineteen Lizzie Coggeshall, whose father, George Folger Coggeshall, was the keeper during the Civil War, wrote to her Cousin Henry expressing her restlessness and loneliness:

> Nantucket   June 15, 1862
> Dear Coz Henry
>
> *I was very much disappointed when I opened your letter, not to find your picture. I think if you knew what a comfort it is to look at my friends, when I am out to the Point, and get entirely tired of seeing the faces of my family, you would send it. I think I shall retain the looks of the family as I had them before me so long. As regards the assistant keeper I would say he is very pleasant, but I think when father is removed from the point, I shall have served an apprenticeship at lightkeeping as long as I care to. You think my experience in household affairs is very limited, but I will assure you I do not care to know more about this house keeping than I already do.*
>
> *I am disgusted with this war for I can't see that we gain one inch of ground. I wish I was a man that I could go to see what was going on, for we don't hear anything here.*
>
> *Grandma is at the point.*
>
> *I think Uncle Hiram will be of more consequence than ever if he returns. I think Liz C. is going to write today, so perhaps between us you may hear something. I am going home next week. I think I shall take my friend Mary Frank with me.*
>
> *It has been raining hard all morning but the sun seems to be trying to shine. We have had it very cold here, yesterday being the only on-comfortably [sic] warm day we have had this season. I have a photograph of Aunt Susan, and one of Aunt Martha. I will tell Aunt Sue about the photograph for you, but think it doubtful whether you get hers unless you send yours. I hope I shall get one, in my next letter from you. I have been writing all the morning, and have got another letter to write, after this. Don't disappoint me. Remember me to your family, if you please.*
>
> Coz Lizzie

Others found life at the light more to their liking. Bill Grieder, whose father Frank kept the Great Point Light from 1934 to 1937, recalls living in town during the week to go to school and then returning home to the lighthouse on weekends, weather permitting. He also enjoyed summers at Great Point before his father's transfer to Gay Head Light on Martha's Vineyard. His mother later won a measure of fame for complaining directly to President Truman about Gay Head's lack of electricity and indoor plumbing.

In April of 1945 Jeannette Lee Haskins wrote this letter about her life as the child of a lightkeeper. Her father, Archford Haskins, came to Great Point from Boston Light in 1937 and later went on to be Assistant Keeper of Sankaty Head Lighthouse. Eighty-three years and a universe of feeling separate her thoughts from those of Lizzie Coggeshall:

> *When I was twelve years old we came to Nantucket to live. My father became keeper of Great Point Light Station. At first sight of the place I was disappointed for Dad had promised us high dunes to slide on and all I could see was coarse beach grass and sand. However, Great Point and the Haskins became fast friends and we liked it much better than any other place we have been. One thing that I did not mention was that we had no modern conveniences and when we moved to Sankaty Light (our present home) we appreciated them as others could not because they are taken so much for granted.*

> *Great Point was a steady light and the tower was shorter than that of Boston Light. Where Boston seemed stately, Great Point seemed "squat" but it seemed to make the station cozy with the house nestled right beneath it. A road led down from the dunes right into our yard and whenever I took a walk I came back that road and stopped on the hill to look at the place I called "Home." The whole station sat in a little valley with dunes all around it. The house was tall, old-fashioned and homey and the tower was nicely shaped. If you are interested in towers you always notice their structure and shape. The whole situation was cozy and neat and we had a very pretty, green lawn which was surprising to see, entirely surrounded by beach grass and sand.*

> *For a few years we had to go to board to go to school and then Dad bought a car and took us in every day and came after us in the afternoon. War stopped that, and we took a house in town. Mom, however, did not like it and neither did we and that summer we went back only to be transferred again to Sankaty Light on the same island. First I will tell you more of Great Point. I always loved storms and still do. The storms there are beautiful. The wind swept along the dunes and at the top of the house, but never came low in our little valley. I used to love to walk in the brisk wind along the beach and feel*

the sting of the sand. I was never lonely. I liked housework and there was always plenty to do. I learned to cook and sew. I found other things to do too. My sister and I collected shells and different things on the beach and made necklaces and bracelets. I used to love to take a book and read under the scrub cedars we called the woods and my sister and I used to lie on top of the boughs watching the sky and look at the sky and talk. Many kinds of flowers grew there too. We were always taking them home to Mom. Every night after supper Dad and Mom used to come outdoor and play with us, croquet, baseball or anything. We were a large, happy family and enjoyed each other and were dependent upon each other for companionship.

Great Point Lighthouse in the automobile era. The walkway has been removed. Note the privy to the left of the dwelling.

We have only been at Sankaty Light since August 1944. As yet we are getting acquainted and in the future I may be able to say, "This I like best of all" but I think we all left part of our hearts at Great Point.

It is strange how I feel about God too. Living as I have has influenced my belief. We have never had a chance to attend church regularly but when I look at all the beautiful things of nature I feel my religion lies there. I feel that such a service as the lighthouse has something to do with God. When men are lost at sea most of them pray for light and when the light is seen it might be a beacon guiding these men back to shore and life. When I light the light (which I do sometimes) I feel as if I am believing and helping God.

There are many advantages to this life, the most important being that you learn about your own. Our family have [sic] so much fun together that outsiders might think it an act except for its sincerity. My sister and I, although there is almost four years between us, get along fine. We never, never quarrel now and I can even remember the last time we did which was over three years ago. That is hard to credit, but true. We try to respect each other's wishes and get fun from each other by making fun. No matter where I go the best moment of all is when I come back home.

In writing this I find there are so many things that I have left out. It is hard to put into words about the things that leave you spellbound such as the first flight of birds north, the first fish found in the lagoon, the first robin on the lawn, but they all go to make up a life you can look back on as being lived to the fullest.

The end of World War II signaled the beginning of the end for manned lighthouses. The position of lighthouse keeper at Great Point was discontinued shortly after the war, as the light had been reconfigured in 1944 to operate using batteries as the power source. The 12,000-candlepower electric fixed white beam was accompanied by a 3500-candlepower red sector. Great Point had always shown a fixed light, but the continuing confusion with nearby lightships had been helped partially when the distinctive red sector was added in 1889 to mark the Cross Rip and Tuckernuck Shoal area; wrecks were reduced but not eliminated.

The lightkeeper's house at Great Point, long since abandoned, burned down at the hands of vandals during the night of October 23, 1966, leaving only the lonely tower with its automated light on remote Great Point.

Great Point has continued to attract its share of human visitors, however. After the demise of the whale fishery, many Nantucketers made their living fishing the waters around the island. The fishing on the island's eastern shore was particularly good, and many fishermen lived in the shanties of Wauwinet and

KAREN T. BUTLER

Brant Point Lighthouse in fog, 1990.

The two remaining Brant Point Lighthouse towers can be seen behind this 1995 reunion of lifesaving vessels. At left, the Nantucket Life Saving Museum's restored surf boat typifies the small craft used by the Life Saving Service. CG36500 is a 1938 self-righting motor lifeboat, while the two vessels on the right

represent the current generation of Coast Guard motor lifeboats: CG44398, built in 1971, is on active duty at Brant Point, while the larger CG47205, a prototype for future Coast Guard rescue vessels, is based in Gloucester, Massachusetts. UNITED STATES COAST GUARD

WILLIAM DICKSON

Nantucketers have long taken their living from the sea. Dories like this were once "basic transportation"
for seafarers up and down New England's coast.

Roy Bailey, "Brant Point" (1992)

Drawn by J. W. Barber—Engraved by S. E. Brown, Boston.
SOUTH-EASTERN VIEW OF NANTUCKET, MASS.

By 1840, Nantucket's economic development as a seaport had peaked. The seventh Brant Point Lighthouse is at the far right of this engraving based on a drawing by J.W. Barber. Great Point is in the distance. Note also the number of steeples that marked the town.

Collection of Karen T. Butler

Brant Point was once home to an active shipbuilding industry, as this James Walter Folger painting, "A View of Brant Point and Entrance to the Harbor at Nantucket, 1820-1842," shows. Note also the whaling ship being towed into harbor atop the "Camels."

Pacific National Bank—Egan Collection

Karen T. Butler

Brant Point Serenity

Brant Point Lighthouse has long been a symbol of welcome to visitors and native islanders alike.
Collection of Karen T. Butler

KAREN T. BUTLER

The 1901 Brant Point Lighthouse continues to greet visitors. Nantucket Town serves as a backdrop for this photograph from a Steamship Authority ferry.

KAREN T. BUTLER

Early risers favored by a Brant Point calm.

David Bareford, "Summer Sail, Brant Point" (1992)

The adage that pennies tossed overboard at Brant Point will guarantee a return to Nantucket applies to everyone, as this humorous 1972 poster by George Davis suggests.

Collection of Anthony B. Cahill

Karen T. Butler

Brant Point Lighthouse, an artist's delight.

Jack Weinhold

Brant Point's light

Nantucket's lighthouses are part of the island's essence, as seen here in "Nantucket," (1986), by Sybil Goldsmith.

John Austin, "Brant Point II" (1985)

Thomas Birch's "Panorama of Nantucket Town from across the Harbor," c. 1810, with the sixth Brant Point Lighthouse visible just to the left of the approaching ship. The 1785 Great Point Light is in the distant background.

Nantucket Historical Association

George C. Thomas, "A Day at Great Point," (1993)

ZELDA B. CAHILL

The 1818 Great Point Lighthouse in the 1970s.

The storm of March 29, 1984 brought the old Great Point tower down on itself. The top of the tower was found buried in the sand some distance away.
Nantucket Life Saving Museum

The concrete core of the rebuilt Great Point Lighthouse nearing completion. Stone work has begun at the base.
Collection of Jane Lamb

Reconstruction underway! A hundred yards northwest (and inland) of the original site, the Great Point Lighthouse rises again in 1985. The rubblestone exterior nearly covers the concrete inner tower at this stage. The new lantern top awaits installation.

Collection of Jane Lamb

The light mechanism at Great Point. The red window panes create the "red sector" that warns mariners of dangerous shoals to the westward.
Collection of Jane Lamb

KAREN T. BUTLER

The new Great Point Lighthouse.

Wrapped in a bright red bow, the newly rebuilt Great Point Lighthouse stands ready to resume work in 1985. The temporary beacon on the left was removed shortly after.

Nantucket Life Saving Museum

Sybil Goldsmith, "Sankaty Light" (1983)

Their facts are incorrect, but the Granger Tobacco Company chose Sankaty Head Lighthouse keeper Eugene Norman Larsen (their spelling was wrong, too) as their model of a pipe-smoking man. Keeper Larsen was concerned that his supervisor would disapprove of the advertisement, but the latter's only question was "Why weren't you wearing your necktie?"

Collection of Ethel Larsen Hamilton

Detail of an 1885 painting of Sankaty Head by W. Ferdinand Macy.

Nantucket Historical Association

KAREN T. BUTLER

Sankaty Head Lighthouse in a summer fog.

Robert Perrin, "Save Sankaty" (1985)

KAREN T. BUTLER

The sea continues to eat away at Sankaty Head bluff. Efforts to protect the lighthouse have proceeded by fits and starts, but those who love the light and its romantic setting are working to make sure that the lighthouse does not go the way of this fence.

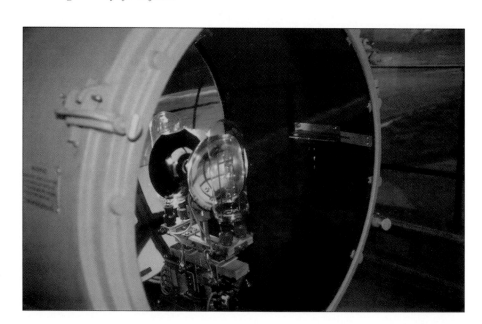

KAREN T. BUTLER

The modern air-sea beacon at Sankaty Head Lighthouse casts a beam powerful enough to be used by aircraft as well as ships.

The red steel hull of Nantucket Lightship No. 117 was no match for the 46,000 tons of the liner Olympic, *which ran the lightship down and sank her on the morning of May 15, 1934. The painting, "Lightship Nantucket Sunk by R.M.S. Olympic" by Charles Mazoujian, was commissioned by the Coast Guard as part of the United States Bicentennial in 1976.*

United States Coast Guard (with permission of the artist)

This Nantucket Lightship of the 1970s represents the zenith of a technology soon to be obsolete. The low tan stack of one of the last Nantucket lightships identifies her as a diesel-powered vessel in Coast Guard (not Lighthouse Service) service, while a huge breakwater forward of her superstructure diverts waves crossing her otherwise fairly unencumbered decks. She floats high in the water, with plenty of reserve buoyancy, and her masts bristle with signal and communication gear.

United States Coast Guard

KAREN T. BUTLER

A floating museum and ambassador of good will, Nantucket Lightship No. 112 visits Nantucket in the summer of 1995. Maintained by a volunteer crew, she operates as a traveling exhibit of the Intrepid Museum in New York City.

Marshall DuBock, "Nantucket Lightship WLV-534." This 1977 print honors the men who worked to preserve the lightship—better known as 112—after she was decommissioned. Known as the "Dirty Dozen," they sailed the lightship home to Nantucket after her brief stint on exhibit in Maine. Manning her on that memorable voyage were Mitchell Todd, Jr., Captain/Navigator; Kenneth Holdgate, Sr., Chief Engineer; Arthur B. Grant, Captain/Navigator; Anthony Docca, Chief Chef; Thomas Eldridge, Captain/Navigator; Richard Mack, Electronic Tech/Helm; Roy Stewart, MD, Asst. Chef/Medical; Jeffrey Marks, Electrician/Helm; Dennis Dias, Jr., Engineer; Richard Hardy, Electrician/Engineer; Robert Allen, Engineer; Daniel Kelliher, Jr., Helm/Ship's Writer.

"The Lightship and the Shamrock" (1995) by Paul Arsenault contrasts the forms of the lightship and the great America's Cup racer of the 1930s.

The "little valley" in which generations of Great Point lightkeeping families lived. Indoor plumbing had arrived by the time this photograph was taken.

Codfish Park in 'Sconset during the summer fishing season. As tourists started to "find" Nantucket and the island became a full-blown summer resort near the turn of the century, it was only natural that they, too, would be attracted by the abundance of fish in the area, and beach fishing at Great Point became very popular. After World War II it was not uncommon for people to catch sharks from the beach at Great Point. Some particularly daring shark fishermen would even don white pants and a white shirt to attract sharks, wading into the rip with long knives to stab the fish. If they happened to attract more than one shark at a time, this recreation could take on a special excitement.

When the second Great Point Lighthouse was built in 1818, it stood a considerable distance from the eastern shore of the point. The seas constantly scoured the site, and wind and surf gnawed away at the sands around the lighthouse, moving them steadily westward. Over time, Great Point Lighthouse would be found sitting on the very edge of the eastern shore, vulnerable to the powerful Atlantic.

As early as 1968, warnings were voiced of the need to save Great Point Lighthouse. People went through the motions of exploring solutions, but a consensus was never achieved. There was much rhetoric, and no concrete action.

The Coast Guard had long taken the position that moving the lighthouse to a safer location would

The 1818 tower of Great Point Lighthouse shortly before its collapse in 1984. The keeper's dwelling had been the victim of a fire set by vandals in 1966.

be too costly; a 1981 estimate came to $450,000. The Coast Guard wanted to protect the light, but the funds were not readily available, as budgeting for such projects was strictly prioritized. As it turned out, funds for the project were not forthcoming in time to save the lighthouse.

Great Point Lighthouse, which had shone so reliably for 167 years, was finally undermined and toppled by the stormy seas, crumbling straight down into a heap of stone. It happened without witnesses some time during the night of March 29, 1984, at the height of a severe Northeaster that packed hurricane-force winds. The collapse was not discovered until the next morning, when it was spotted from the air; a portion of the base of the tower and a pile of rubble were all that remained of what had once been the steadfast Great Point Lighthouse.

The news of the collapse was met with disbelief and then profound sadness, as word of Great Point's abrupt demise traveled around the island and to lovers of Nantucket's proud old lighthouse everywhere. Many theories circulated about the actual cause of the fall of the Great Point tower. One of them was espoused by Mildred Jewett (known affectionately as "Madaket Millie"), an honorary Coast Guard member who continued to run Nantucket's

Remnants of the 1984 collapse of the 1818 Great Point Lighthouse.

The new Great Point tower nears completion.

Madaket Coast Guard Station long after its official closing. She maintained that moisture had accumulated within the walls of the tower from heavy rains that night. She theorized that lightning struck the lighthouse, exploding the tower and sending the lighthouse crashing to the ground. The top of the lighthouse was found buried deep in sand not far from the pile of rubble.

Most people thought that erosion had simply undermined the foundation and that the ultimate blow was the heavy winds and the strong undertow that momentous night. The lighthouse, which in 1984 stood less than ten feet above sea level and about thirty feet from the shoreline, was pounded by ninety mile-an-hour winds and powerful fifteen- to twenty-foot waves. It was one more victory for the weather; storms have destroyed more lighthouses in New England than in any other region of the country.

Ironically, just four or five months before the Great Point

A construction crane at work on the new Great Point Lighthouse in 1985.

The lantern top is about all that is needed to finish up work on the new Great Point Lighthouse. The open "window frame" was later fitted with photovoltaic cells to provide the light's electricity.

Lighthouse toppled, the crew of the Coast Guard Cutter *White Sage* had totally refurbished the light, repainting it and otherwise putting it in tip-top shape. Great Point went out in a blaze of glory, "wearing a tuxedo."

Early correspondence showed that the Coast Guard wanted to replace the collapsed lighthouse with an unsightly thirty-three-foot fiberglass tower mounted on a cement base. Nantucketers had already vetoed a proposed steel lattice tower. The notion of a plastic lighthouse was greeted with even more dismay, especially in a locale that had worked harder than most to maintain its historic character.

Ultimately, just under $1,000,000 was spent to construct a replica of the 1818 Great Point Lighthouse, but the reality of the matter was that the original lighthouse was gone. In an historical nicety, funds for the rebuilding were appropriated by means of an amendment to the Continuing Resolution of 1817, which had provided for the construction of the original Great Point Lighthouse.

There were several changes in the reproduction. The new light would be more than eleven feet higher than the original tower, greatly increasing its visibility. The light was also moved west of its original 1818 location to better protect it from erosion. The tower was constructed differently from the original, having a 35-foot-deep foundation, an inner core of reinforced concrete, an exterior surface of rubblestone, and an interior lined with brick. The wrought-iron spiral staircase was recreated in aluminum, and unobtrusive solar cells were installed to power the light.

Visible for fourteen miles at sea, Great Point's seventy-foot white tower is officially designated by the Coast Guard as Nantucket (Great Point) Light (No. 530, formerly No. 13650, on the light list). It shows a 25,000-candlepower fixed white light, flashing a brilliant white every five seconds with a 5,000-candlepower fixed red sector bearing from 84 to 106 degrees. The red sector faces westerly over Cross Rip and Tuckernuck Shoals, and an alert mariner knows he is in danger of running aground when in the shadow of the red sector of Great Point light.

Today, as fishermen and their four-wheel drive vehicles dot the beach, Great Point tower stands sadly alone. No, it is not the tower of old, but its light still beams across the waters to aid mariners along their way. Beneath the tower, the soft dunes with their eel grass slowly wash away into the Atlantic, lost forever to the ceaseless action of the wind and waves. At Great Point nature reigns supreme.

If we let our imagination run, we can look out and see the hundreds of schooners that passed Great Point Lighthouse and the ghosts of many that were caught in the point's greedy rip. Over the years the light has shone impartially on vessels wrecked, cargo foregone, and lives lost. It has also lighted the way for fortunes being carried home from the South Seas and for the more mundane treasures of a growing nation. Whalers, fishermen, yachtsmen, and traders, Great Point has stood by for all, knowing steadfastness and valor, destruction and loss.

Chapter Four

"O, BLAZING STAR!"
SANKATY HEAD LIGHTHOUSE

. . . a high cliff overhanging the sea and crowned with a pasture for sheep; a little way off--higher up--a light-house. . . . The afternoon is mild and warm. The sea with an air of solemn deliberation, with an elaborate deliberation, ceremoniously rolls upon the beach. The air is suppressedly charged with the sound of long lines of surf. There is no land over against this cliff short of Europe and the West Indies . . . along the cliff . . . the continual assaults of the sea have undermined it; so that the fences fall over and have many shiftings inland. The sea has encroached also upon that part where their dwelling-house stands near the light-house . . . in strange and beautiful contrast, we have the innocence of the land eyeing the malignity of the sea.

--Herman Melville, in a letter to Nathaniel Hawthorne written after a visit to Sankaty Head (1852)

In 1847 Lieutenant Charles Davis of the U. S. Navy discovered a dangerous reef, soon to be named Davis's South Shoals, while taking soundings off the eastern shore of Nantucket. He strongly urged that a lighthouse be built to warn mariners of the hazard, recommending the high bluff of Sankaty Head, a mile and a half north of Siasconset, as the site.

Sankaty, Sankoty, Sancoty, or Sankata—as the area at the extreme east end of Nantucket Island has been variously spelled—was also called "Naphchecoy," meaning "around the head." Sankaty may have been the prominent headland sighted by the crew of the English explorer George Weymouth in 1605; if so, Weymouth's men are

Looking south toward Sankaty Head Lighthouse in the 1930s.

Nantucket's European "discoverers." There is a tradition that a French treasure ship had been the first European vessel to come to grief off that coast. The ship was lost, according to the story, but the survivors received food and shelter from native islanders living nearby in a dense forest. Legends of buried treasure from the ship persisted, but in the course of years of searching none was found.

In 1848 Congress responded to Davis's recommendation with an appropriation of $12,000 for the construction of a lighthouse at Sankaty Head, and a year later building began. The site of New England's southeasternmost lighthouse was near the edge of a cliff about a hundred feet above the ocean, farther at sea than any Atlantic coast lighthouse station.

Transporting all the bricks, granite blocks, and other building materials to Nantucket by schooner, Cabot King, a Hingham, Massachusetts, contractor, built the original sixty-foot tower of brick topped with a granite turret for $10,330.

In addition, Sankaty Head was the beneficiary of the government's desire to significantly improve America's lighthouse system. By 1850 the Fresnel lens, developed in 1822 by the French scientist Augustin Fresnel, had been widely and enthusiastically used in Europe, but resistance to change had slowed acceptance of the lens on this side of the Atlantic. But at last the Lighthouse Establishment was willing to make substantial investments in aids to navigation, and Sankaty Head was to be America's first lighthouse built with Fresnel's lens as original equipment.

Benjamin Isherwood, who later became chief engineer for the U.S. Navy during the Civil War, was sent to France by the government to supervise the manufacture of a state-of-the-art Fresnel lens for this lighthouse. The lens, made by Henri Lepaute of Paris at a cost of $10,000, remained in use at Sankaty for over a century. Isherwood also oversaw the installation of the lens, with its complex and delicate assembly of bull's-eyes and prisms. Later, the Fresnel system pioneered at Sankaty proved successful enough to be used throughout the national lighthouse system.

Shaped like a large beehive surrounding a single lamp, the Fresnel lens had prisms at the top and bottom that bent the light, preventing it from diffusing. Instead, the prisms and magnifying glass multiplied the intensity of the light by drawing it together in a very narrow band. In the Sankaty light, the large center lens emitted the intense "flash" while smaller prisms provided the constant light. The brilliant, concentrated light of the flash was visible for distances unthinkable before the use of the Fresnel lens.

The lens itself was on a platform turned by a clockwork apparatus with heavy weights suspended inside the lighthouse tower on wire cable. The falling weights slowly unwound the wire cable, rotating the

The advances in lens design made by Augustin Fresnel in the early nineteenth century made possible a revolution in lighthouse design—and safety at sea.

light on its turntable. For eighty-eight years the mechanism had to be wound several times a day by the lightkeepers, until an electric motor was installed in 1938.

Sankaty, poetically hailed as the "Blazing Star," was fitted with a second-order lens, the second most powerful that Fresnel could build. Half-inch-thick glass encased in brass and bronze frames protected the lens from fierce winds or the occasional sea-bird attracted to the light in error. Shades were drawn around the lantern during the day to protect the lens from discoloration by the sun's rays.

The original four-foot-tall lamp within the Fresnel lens was brilliant enough to be seen twenty miles out at sea. A weight-driven piston that had to be wound frequently forced oil up a pipe into a wick chamber. Four concentric wicks produced one solid mass of flame. Unburned oil drained back into the reservoir, acting as a coolant to keep the intense heat from damaging the lamp. This "single-wick" whale oil lamp consumed 395 gallons of oil a year.

Sankaty was illuminated for the very first time on the first day of February in 1850. Blazing 158 feet above

Sankaty Head Lighthouse in the early 1930s.

sea level, the beam from Sankaty's red-banded white tower at first showed a fixed light interspersed at set intervals by a brilliant white flash. Today the light emits a brilliant white flash of 3,200,000 candlepower every seven and a half seconds, visible at night for twenty-four miles. At times the light has been seen at even greater distances due to reflection of the beam off clouds.

The original single-wick whale-oil lamp in the light was later replaced by a lamp with several wicks, and after that with a kerosene-vapor light that increased the candlepower to 99,000. Electrification of the rotating mechanism on May 15, 1933, allowed the keeper, for the first time, to sleep through the night. An electric light installed at the same time raised the level of illumination to 720,000 candlepower, later intensified to 1.1 million. With electrification Sankaty Head Lighthouse also became a one-keeper station; previously an assistant keeper had been needed.

Sankaty Head Lighthouse, its superbly constructed tower having lasted to the present day, was a model in its time: state-of-the-art in every way. In 1852 the Lighthouse Board reported that Sankaty was the best-built and best-performing light in New England. A committee authorized by Congress to investigate the lighthouse system stated that Sankaty Head, with its second-order Fresnel lens, was one of the two best lights on the coast of the United States. The report found that the Fresnel lens was four times more effective than the Argand lamps with reflectors in use in most American lighthouses at that time. The report

stipulated that the Fresnel lens be used in all new lighthouses and in any lights being renovated.

The report concluded, "The Lights of France, England, Scotland, Ireland and those of the maritime nations of Europe in general . . . are far superior to those on the coast of the United States . . . . The other aids to navigation consisting of floating lights, beacons, buoys, range marks, etc. are kept up in a more efficient manner than they are in this country." The report also felt that American lights looked too much alike to sailors at sea. Those strong criticisms led to the establishment of the Lighthouse Board on August 31, 1852, heralding a new era for America's lighthouses and lightships, and by the time the Civil War began, every lighthouse in the United States had a Fresnel lens similar to the one Sankaty had pioneered.

Sankaty's is a seacoast light, highlighting trouble with its far-reaching beam, in contrast to the welcoming harbor light at Brant Point. It is not difficult for a mariner to become disoriented in the open Atlantic, and on numerous occasions Sankaty was confused with Gay Head Lighthouse on Martha's Vineyard or Nantucket's Great Point. To mistake Sankaty's flashing light for Gay Head's could lead to a grounding, or worse, on Nantucket's south shore.

The first man entrusted with the responsibility of keeping Sankaty Head Lighthouse was a highly respected and successful retired shipmaster, Captain Alex Bunker. He and his two assistants kept four-hour watches at the light, trimming the wick to maximize

The original brick keeper's dwelling at Sankaty, forming an "ell" with the tower so as to provide some relief from high winds. The people in the photograph remain unidentified.

the light's brightness and tending the various mechanisms that operated the light—work on which the lives of fellow mariners depended. Along with the endless cycle of routine chores, the making of numerous trips up and down the many stairs of the lighthouse added to the demanding nature of the job. Winding and trimming at night and cleaning and polishing the lens by day, the keeper could never stray far from the lighthouse, and so a dwelling for him was built adjacent to the tower.

During the day the red and white tower of the Sankaty light served as a landmark, but its reliability at night was the essence of its role. One early advance involved the installation of an "English wick" at Sankaty, enabling the lightkeeper to trim the wicks only once during the night, an improvement over the two or three trimmings previously required. The keeper kept a daily log, recording the weather and adding remarks pertinent to the keeping of the light. Most of the time those remarks reflect the repetitious and routine nature of life at the light.

The landmark status of the light extended shoreward as well, and Sankaty Head became an attractive destination for summer picnics and those seeking the fun of climbing the lighthouse tower. From its heights one could enjoy a spectacular vista that encompassed the island of Nantucket, the beautiful blue of the Atlantic to the east, the petite cottages of 'Sconset to the south, and the undulating brown and purple moors to the west. The lighthouse was so popular that

in 1856 the platform near the top of the lighthouse was widened to allow ladies wearing hoopskirts to marvel at both the Fresnel lens and the breath-taking view.

Visitors to Nantucket enjoyed the beauty of Sankaty Head Lighthouse, but its keepers, most of whom had come to the job with years of experience at sea, found it a strict taskmaster. The Lighthouse Board sought reliable men who had some maritime knowledge, yet who could handle the repetitive nature of the job. They had to make daily entries in their logs, fix whatever was in need of repair, and be fastidious enough to be prepared for inspection by their superiors. For an inspection, polishing brass was the order of the day; even the dustpan at the lighthouse was made of brass and had to be polished. The Lighthouse Board prepared a manual of "laws relating to the light-house service," each of which had to be followed precisely.

For lightkeepers with families, the challenges of making a lighthouse a fit place to live were considerable. Drinking water could be a problem, so cisterns were built within the tower base, and an official circular from the Lighthouse Board advised them to avoid drinking water that dripped from leaded roofs, gutters, or seams. They were instructed to put powdered chalk into the cistern and stir occasionally, a rather simplistic solution to a potential health threat. In addition to the water dilemma, cattle ate dune grass, causing erosion; birds hit lights and broke glass during storms. The items of food and clothing needed for everyday living were not always easily accessible.

REGULATIONS IN REGARD TO PROVISIONS FOR LIGHT-HOUSE KEEPERS, OFFICERS, AND CREWS OF LIGHT-HOUSE VESSELS.

181. *Table of weekly allowance per man for vessels of the Light-House Establishment.*

Beef (corned)	1 pound.	Molasses	½ pint.
Pork	2 pounds.	Coffee	7 ounces.
Codfish	1 pound.	Tea	1¾ ounces.
Mutton (fresh canned)	1 pound.	Butter	8 ounces.
Bacon	1 pound.	Vinegar	½ pint.
Ham	1 pound.	Pickles	½ pound.
Flour	4 pounds.	Tomatoes (canned)	8 ounces.
Pilot bread	2 pounds.	Corn (canned)	8 ounces.
Rice	¼ pound.	Apples (evaporated)	2 ounces.
Corn meal	½ pound.	Peaches (dried)	2 ounces.
Oatmeal	¼ pound.	Raisins	1 ounce.
Beans	1 pint.	Salt	6 ounces.
Pease (split)	½ pint.	Pepper	¼ ounce.
Potatoes	12 pounds.	Mustard	¼ ounce.
Onions	2 pounds.	Baking powder	1 ounce.
Sugar	2 pounds.		

182. *Table of annual allowance per man for light-stations and fog-signal stations.*

Pork	200 pounds.	Coffee (green grain)	24 pounds.
Beef	100 pounds.	Beans or pease	10 gallons.
Flour	2 barrels.	Vinegar	4 gallons.
Rice	50 pounds.	Potatoes	2 barrels.
Brown sugar	50 pounds.		

183. Salt provisions and the other articles embraced in the ration list should be put on board in quarterly quantities, and at or near the beginning of each quarter year, deducting, as near as may be estimated, the quantities of each article of pork and beef, etc., which may be substituted by fresh meat and green vegetables during the quarter.

What the proper lighthouse should have on hand and how it should be run were strictly prescribed by the Lighthouse Board. The 1902 regulations are astonishingly detailed.

The Lighthouse Board's manual outlined what equipment should be on hand at any lighthouse, specifying quantities as well: how many wicks, how many glass chimneys for the lamps, how much of the cleaning materials for the lens. Keepers were issued buff or chamois skins for lens polishing and linen towels marked "United States Light-House Establishment," and they were warned not to use the items for personal cleaning. They received spirits of wine (distilled alcohol) for washing lenses, hickory brooms, and corn brooms. The Board apportioned how much paint and turpentine each light station would receive. Keepers were given only one journal a year for their daily entries and six pages a year to make shipwreck reports. The manual also details how and when each supply should be used and how every duty should be performed.

In November 1861 the Secretary of the Lighthouse Board, Thornton A. Jenkins, sent this reminder to all lighthouse keepers to help them

> *to perform efficiently all the duties required of them by the printed instructions and directions for keeping bright and steady lights, and in keeping their lanterns, light-room towers, and dwellings clean and neat.*
>
> *Unless the illuminating apparatus, lamps, and lantern-glass of a light-house are kept clean and in good condition, a good light cannot be produced, and mariners will complain. . . .*
>
> *The glass of the lantern must be washed as often as necessary to keep it clean and free from stains of every kind. LINEN TOWELS ONLY ARE TO BE USED IN WIPING the glass of the lens and the plate-glass of the lantern, as the finest cotton when rubbed against glass will scratch it.*
>
> *The curtains of the lantern must be put up, or the lens cover must be put on (particularly in clear weather) before sunrise, and one or the other must protect the lamp in the lens by shutting out the sun's rays in this way during the whole day. It will be best, as a general rule, to put up the curtains before sunrise.*
>
> *After extinguishing the light in the morning, the lens, before the operation of cleaning it is commenced, should be dusted with a feather brush, to remove any dust which may have accumulated upon it, and which, if left upon it while it is cleaned with rouge and spirits of wine, will scratch and injure it. . . .*
>
> *The light-keepers and their assistants are provided with linen aprons to put on over their clothes while engaged in the lanterns cleaning them, and the illuminating apparatus. These aprons will be delivered to the principal keepers, who alone will be responsible for them. The assistants will retain possession of those for their use while at the light stations, but when they leave they must turn them over to the principal keepers. . . .*

Sesachacha Pond lies in the background as this gathering of men (and a horse and buggy) enjoy what appears to be a tranquil nineteenth century day at Sankaty Head Lighthouse.

Lightkeeper Joseph Remsen and his family in 1906. Keeper Remsen spent 27 years at Sankaty Head, having already been keeper at Brant Point and master of the Nantucket Lightship. To his credit, all seven of Remsen's assistant keepers went on to become keepers of New England lighthouses.

Light-keepers will be careful to see that all articles called for by the receipts are actually landed from the supply-vessel or otherwise, and all articles to be put in fixed places of deposit, are so to be delivered. The oil must be measured and put in the butts, and the casks returned to the vessel; and all small articles must be put into the properly marked or labeled tin boxes, &c.

Improvements to the lighthouse and the keeper's dwelling continued. The height of the Sankaty lighthouse was increased to seventy feet in 1883 with the installation of a new deck, which was more like a balcony. In 1886 telephones and a telegraph line were installed. The next year the original keeper's house was razed and a new two-family dwelling for the keeper and his assistant was erected at a cost of $6,700.

Sankaty Head Lighthouse in 1947, with some outbuildings undergoing demolition; the guardhouses on the bluff date from the World War II era.

In 1888 Wallace A. Eldridge became assistant keeper at Sankaty Head Lighthouse, where he served for fourteen years. Island-born, Eldridge got the job because his brother-in-law was a figure in Democratic politics; patronage appointments were common in the era of the Lighthouse Board. He described the work of lightkeeper as requiring "unceasing regularity," summer and winter, never giving into illness.

There were, however, moments of grave drama and impending tragedy, including the famous wreck of the three-masted schooner *H. P. Kirkham* on Rose and Crown Shoal off Nantucket before dawn on the wintry day of January 20th, 1892. Joseph Remsen, the alert head lighthouse keeper, notified the Coskata Life Saving Station of a vessel off shore burning torches, a signal of distress. The Coskata crew, led by Walter Nelson Chase, rowed their lifeboat about ten miles to the sinking schooner in a freezing gale and took on board the seven men who had been stranded on the partially submerged vessel for many hours.

Their return journey proved to be a Herculean struggle with the sea. Although they could see the top of Sankaty Head Lighthouse, they were rowing against the wind and tide. The overcrowded lifeboat required frantic bailing to keep from swamping, as the oarsmen struggled with treacherous cross seas and an outgoing tide. Twice they anchored for many hours in the bitter cold, waiting for the tide to turn and ease their rowing. Miraculously they endured through the long and desperate night on the rough Atlantic, making 'Sconset at ten the next morning. The brave Coskata Life Saving crew had been at sea for twenty-six hours, saving all on board the *H. P. Kirkham.* It was later learned that the men on the *Kirkham* had used bed-clothing soaked in kerosene as torches to signal for help. The U. S. Government awarded medals to Walter Chase and the other members of heroic Coskata Life Saving crew at a ceremony held at the Unitarian Church on January 9, 1893 (see sidebar).

Such dramas were, fortunately, rare on the Sankaty shore. Sankaty Head was more often the scene of more peaceful

A RESCUE COMMEMORATED

The rescue of the crew of the *H. P. Kirkham* was commemorated in a poem by the Rev. Louise S. Baker published in 1893 in her book, *By the Sea*:

THE LIFE-BOAT

The night fell swift and sure upon our island coasts.
All dark and peaceful lay the old, gray-shingled town,
Save where the glimmering lights chased off the windy ghosts
Of shadows playing here and yonder, roughly blown.

Then one by one these flickered out and desolate
The gloom that gathered while the unconscious people slept.
Brant Light and Great Point lit the waters wide, while fate
Its path pursued, and on the ocean white waves crept.

Sleep on, all dreamless, ye who dwell within your doors!
A watch is in the tower, one keeps the lonely street,
While heroes bravely guard your long, outlying shores,
And through the dreary night the patrol holds his beat.

No vision in your dreams of wintry seas, nor sight
Of yonder boat upon its devious, toilsome way,
That left its station on the beach in dull twilight
Soon after day-dawn broke the dark to fragments gray.

E'er since the morning swept the shore, this little bark
Has bravely fought in rescue, dared the biting cold,
And famished hours manned by a royal crew with mark
Of coronation on their brows brighter than gold.

Yon dangerous shoal a vessel clutched within its maw.
And there the little life-boat slowly made its way,
Gathered its precious burden from the hungry jaw
Of death, and headed homeward through the sharp noon-day.

continued on page 79

occurrences, the day-to-day adventures of families making do in one of the coastal frontier's most colorful settings. This 1899 letter to the *Inquirer and Mirror* recounts those times:

> *"No more waifs from Sankoty," said a former keeper of its lighthouse, a few days ago. He referred pleasantly to a correspondence of mine, a weekly budget of notes that I used to mail to* THE INQUIRER AND MIRROR, *long years ago. Those were halcyon days. My grandfather, the late Capt. Henry Winslow, was then princi-*

> *pal keeper at Sankoty Head. It was a breezy bluff, ninety feet above the sea-level. From the rich brown summit of the mossy headland I could just discern the white tower of Great Point lighthouse. Between me and the distant sandy dunes, rolled a brilliant expanse of ocean; its sparkle seemed to fire my youthful imagination; the sullen, continual roar of the surf on the beach below me, was typical of what resistless perseverance can achieve; wave following wave taught me how trial after trial surely impels to*

Sankaty stands clearly against the sky on a crisp winter's day.

Sankaty Head Lighthouse from the air in 1953. The experimentally installed surveillance radar stands in front of the light tower.

The U. S. Army Corps of Engineers evaluated the erosion at Sankaty Head in 1989. Their study concluded that relocation of the tower to safer ground would be the best and most cost-effective solution among various proposed measures.

In the 1990s a number of plans have been discussed to "Save Our Sankaty," including moving the 690-ton lighthouse back some 200 feet from its precarious perch, now less than 110 feet from the bluff. In 1992 the Nantucket Historical Association indicated its willingness to coordinate efforts to move the light, but the scale of the project—the estimated cost of the move approached $1 million in 1992—required more resources than the association had available. The 'Sconset Trust has agreed with the Coast Guard to receive ownership of Sankaty Head

Lighthouse, provided that a new erosion-control and beach-nourishment project, which would negate the need to move the lighthouse, is working. That may take several years to determine.

Today, erosion has made it nearly impossible to stand on the bluff close to Sankaty. Much of the cliff east of the light has already slid into the Atlantic Ocean, leaving some to wonder when relentless erosion will claim the lighthouse as Great Point Light succumbed before it.

As it has for nearly a century and a half, Sankaty Head Lighthouse sits on its sandy bluff, resembling a forlorn "waif" in need of love and care, awaiting the next chapter. No one knows what fate the next great Northeaster may bring or whether the forces arrayed to save it will prevail. Whatever its fate—and we trust it will be a happy one—it is appropriate to close this chapter on Nantucket's brightest light with a salute:

O, Blazing Star! May you keep shining over the seas!

This 1944 lithograph of Sankaty by Henry Mitchell Havemeyer shows why the strong forms and stark contrasts of the light have long appealed to artists.

Chapter Five

THE SHIP THAT NEVER SAILED
THE NANTUCKET LIGHTSHIP

Nantucket. Lying as it does directly in the track of vessels plying between the principal American ports north and south of the Island, the waves which . . . break in angry foam upon the shoals and rips nearby, have reaped a harvest of shipwreck and death almost unparalleled upon the American coast.

--Arthur H. Gardner,

Wrecks Around Nantucket (1915)

The romance of America's thousand or so lighthouses continues to fascinate people, and an imperiled lighthouse usually galvanizes public reaction. Rarer still, more intriguing and more in danger of being forgotten forever are the lightships that once formed the first line of security for deep-water shipping. Only a handful, perhaps a dozen, of them are left, none on station; they have long since been replaced by huge mechanical buoys. Among the most famous is the Nantucket Lightship, which, secured by a 7,000-pound anchor and twelve tons of chain, once held her lonely vigil more than forty miles off the coast of the island for which she was named. Homeward bound, the sight of the Nantucket South Shoals Lightship was the sailor's first evidence that the journey was nearing its end; going out, it was the last reminder of home port.

As transatlantic ship traffic increased in the nineteenth century and into our own, the "inshore" coastal route north of Nantucket became largely confined to domestic trade. International trade from the south and east increasingly gravitated to the Port of New York, and so the shipping route to the south of Nantucket became the pathway of America's transoceanic commerce. It was along this route for a century and a quarter that the sight of the Nantucket Lightship assured the mariner that his vessel was 200 miles east of New York and clear of

The Nantucket Lightship wore her name boldly. Glassy calm or raging storm, she held her station with no excuses.

Nantucket's hazardous shoals. The very last of its kind, the Nantucket Lightship held its station until 1979. When the ship was decommissioned four years later, America's lightship era had come to an end.

The shoals and rips to the east and southeast of Nantucket have long been known as posing extreme danger to unsuspecting vessels. In 1835 Obed Macy noted in his *History of Nantucket* that the

> *many shoals to the eastward of the island, and the great South Shoal to the southward, render the navigation difficult and compel those not*

acquainted to keep a safe distance at sea. Although there are no rock ledges, nor rocky shores, around the island, yet it is not infrequent, especially in the winter, that vessels lose their way and are wrecked on some part. Such misfortunes, though causing much destruction of property, are not frequently attended with loss of lives.

When navigating the coastal regions of northeastern North America for any distance, one is always close to menacing shoals. They parallel main shipping

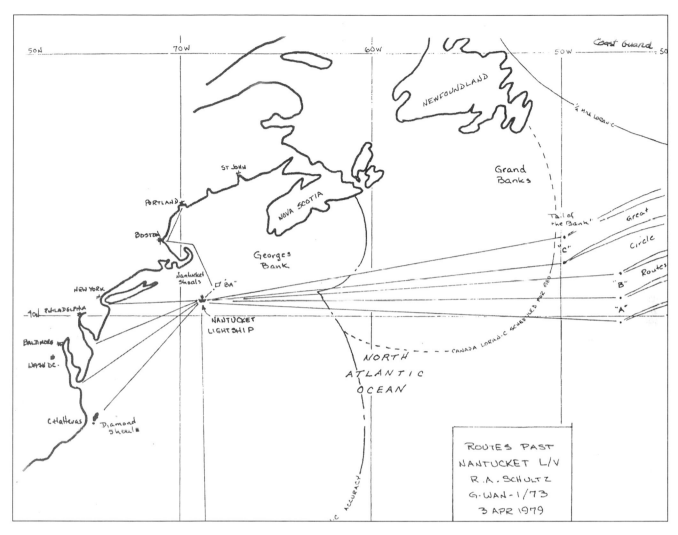

As the Great Circle routes across the North Atlantic converged, the Nantucket Lightship became their focal point. The coastal routes then diverged toward Maine and the Carolinas. Anchored in the middle of traffic and a "target" for radar and radio direction-finders, the Nantucket Lightship risked being rammed at any moment.

channels, patiently waiting for the unwary mariner to stray from his course as a spider waits to catch a fly. The Nantucket shoals, with their swift currents, are especially dangerous. They are as well a place of dense, clinging fogs that obscure vision and prevent the penetration of light beams. To make matters worse, a phenomenon known as acoustic refraction can radically distort the direction from which sound is perceived in such fog. The powerful seas of heavy storms often shift the sands below the surface, changing the configuration of the shoals; even the seasoned mariner can suddenly find himself aground on a shoal that had not previously existed.

The beam of a lighthouse perched on the shore could warn mariners of dangers along the immediate coast, but there were places where building a light-

The liner R.M.S. Olympic *changes course close by the Nantucket Lightship. Her bow wave indicates a sharp turn, producing perhaps an anxious moment for the lightship's crew.*

house was an engineering impossibility. Thus, the need for lightships was apparent. Europeans had been using lightships since the eighteenth century, but their first application in North America was not made until 1820.

What is a lightship? It is simply a vessel fitted with lights and moored at sea at points such as approaches to harbors or in the vicinity of obscure reefs or shoals. Early lightships had only minimal provisions for self-propulsion, being built primarily to absorb the shock of riding out heavy weather at anchor. In a sense, a lightship is a manned buoy. Later lightships on exposed stations had full self-propulsion capability, electric lighting, radio-telegraph communi-

cations equipment, and fog signals. A lightship bears the name of its station on its hull in large markings. It also displays the flags of its station's International Code Signal ("A L A U" for the Nantucket Lightship) when another vessel approaches.

Before 1851 mariners had tried unsuccessfully to persuade Congress to position a lightship off Nantucket Shoals. Congress had even investigated the possibility of building an open-water lighthouse, like England's famed Eddystone, but that more revolutionary (and expensive) idea never took hold.

In 1853 the U. S. Government made the decision to place a lightship to the south of Nantucket, placing a make-shift "Nantucket South Shoals" light-

An early Nantucket Light Vessel hauled for maintenance in Fairhaven, Massachusetts. The distinctive skyline of New Bedford is in the background.

Fog presented a constant hazard to ships approaching Nantucket Lightship No. 112. The diaphone trumpet horn rising vertically from the deckhouse produced a deafening note of warning. The horn was an improvement paid for with funds from the White Star Line's settlement after the Olympic *sank the Nantucket Lightship in 1934. It created great difficulty for the lightship's crew, who were forced to become proficient lip-readers and patient speakers as they adjusted their lives to the regular blast of the horn in foggy weather.*

ship on station the following year. Two years later funds were appropriated to build a new vessel for the task.

The Nantucket Lightship, temporary though it was, went on station in 1854 at Old South Shoal, fourteen miles off Nantucket. As commercial vessels grew in size, warranting deeper shipping channels, the lightship's position moved steadily seaward. Soon it was moved eight miles farther south to Davis South Shoal, and by 1915 the Nantucket Lightship was moored southwest of Asia Rip, forty-three miles south-southeast of Sankaty Head. Land was visible to the lightship crews from all but the last station.

Life on the Nantucket Lightship was one of agonizing monotony punctuated by moments of terror. Most of the time the lightship rolled placidly on the gentle swells while the crew went about their daily chores. When the weather changed and the seas started to churn, things altered swiftly and dramatically. While

An early solution to the fog problem was the bell—which of course had to be rung by hand at regular intervals. In this 1891 engraving this duty looks less than pleasant.

The heart of a lightship's function. Keeping the lanterns clean and in first-rate working order in all weathers was the crew's chief task.

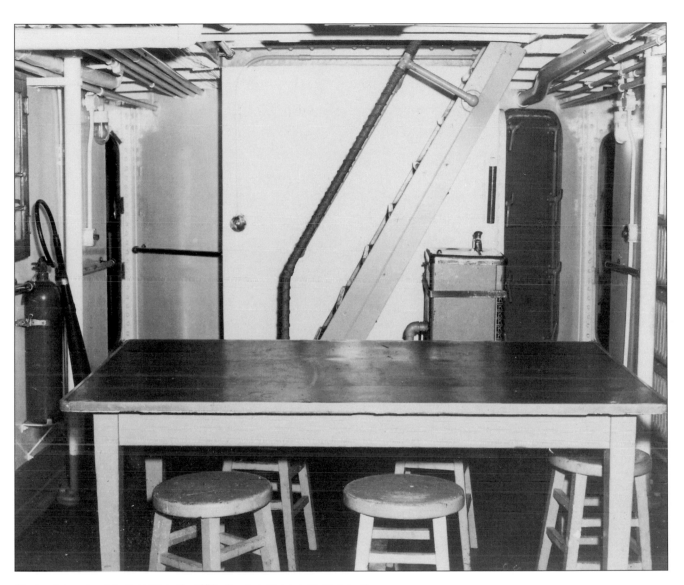

Spartan living aboard the lightship in the 1950s. Pegs in table tops held objects in place.

other ships ran for cover at the first sign of an impending storm, the Nantucket Lightship prepared to endure the worst. In the nineteenth century Northeasters, many of them hurricane force, came as a surprise, for weather forecasting was still primitive. No matter what the circumstances, the lightship was never to leave its station; its commitment was to warn of the dangerous shoals, braving the worst weather imaginable.

The Nantucket South Shoals were a real ocean graveyard, and only an area of such obvious danger warranted subjecting a lightship and its crew to such an exposed position. The Nantucket Lightship was among the loneliest and most isolated in the world.

Being aboard was like standing on a tennis ball in the middle of the ocean, bobbing, pitching, and rolling, endless hour after endless hour. With the area shrouded in pea-soup fog sixty per cent of the time, the crew became accustomed to the bellow of the fog horn's deafening warning. The lightship crew learned to speak to each other in cadence with the horn, breaking their words as the horn would blast.

Duty aboard the Nantucket Lightship, in cramped quarters that offered little privacy and forced intimacy in moments of boredom and fear alike, was only for the strong of mind. The work of the ship, especially when repairs needed to be made in the middle of a gale, was only for the strong of body. Crewmembers of the early lightships were pushed to their mental and physical limits of endurance, alternating four months at sea with two months ashore. Later crews, particularly after the Coast Guard took over lightships in 1939, had much shorter stays. Small ships to begin with, the lightships felt smaller still when storm waves pounded the hull, splashing over the deck and pouring into any apertures. Fog, which increased the likelihood of collision, sometimes lasted for weeks at a time, adding to the feeling of depression and isolation. Lightship duty was regarded by many mariners as the most difficult of all maritime service.

On one occasion, the captain and the first mate of the Nantucket Lightship were so estranged that whenever they sat down for dinner they pulled a curtain between them so they would not have to lay eyes on each other. Most crews, however, were compatible; they had to be, for their own lives and the lives of others depended on their ability to work together under extreme conditions.

The fear of collision was ever present, even with the lights and the horn by which the Nantucket Lightship made its presence known. Ocean-going vessels gradually became faster and heavier, as steam and diesel engines pushed larger and larger iron and steel hulls. Advances in speed and weight added to the terrifying dangers of being stationed on the tiny and stationary Nantucket Lightship, and in later years crews practiced abandon-ship procedures religiously.

Many ship captains traveling in these waters had only the slightest local knowledge. Making their way from port to port, they quickly came to depend on the Nantucket Lightship as a "living buoy" to guide them around the dangerous shoals south of Nantucket.

THE FIRST NANTUCKET LIGHTSHIP: NO. 11—1853

The first Nantucket Lightship was officially assigned the designation of No. 11 by the government. No. 11, with a bluff bow and 104 feet long, was converted in 1853 from an old Nantucket whaling vessel that had become too small for the needs of the time. The old brig was re-rigged as a schooner, the bridge

No. 11, the first—temporary, as it turned out—Nantucket Lightship. Here she is painted for duty on the Scotland station off New Jersey.

and the yardarms removed, and two yellow lantern masts, each seventy feet high, were placed forward of the sailing masts. With "Nantucket South Shoal" painted boldly on her red hull, this makeshift vessel was placed in service on June 15, 1854. The cost to outfit her was $20,000; in 1976 it was estimated that a new lightship would cost $750,000 to construct.

Captain Samuel Bunker, the vessel's first captain, wrote of the weather in his journal after only several weeks on station, where the summer months brought many days of very low visibility. The entries in Capt. Bunker's log read succinctly "fog, fog, fog."

In February of 1855, a strong winter storm blew this improvised Nantucket Lightship off her station, setting her adrift and finally running her aground off Montauk Point. Miraculously, the crew was saved, although the ship was wrecked.

Captain Bunker's journal, demonstrating a true New England penchant for brevity and understatement, tells the story:

THURSDAY 1ST *First Part [of the day] fine weather wind NW Middle Part the "sumes" broke one of our Signal Lanterns one Bark in sight Latter Part fine weather and hazy wind North and smooth so Ends*

FRIDAY 2ND *First Part Moderate and Thick at 6 PM spit of snow weather looking hard overhauled our water found we had about 200 Gallons Middle Part fine clear with light flights of snow Latter Part fresh breezes from NW and cool saw nothing so Ends*

SATURDAY 3RD *First Part fine weather and fresh breezes from NW and cool caught 2 Cod 2 Haddock Middle Part commenced Snowing Latter Part a snow storm wind from West and saw ship standing to the E. ward so Ends*

SUNDAY 4TH *First Part strong breezes from West and clear Middle Part clear wind West a bad sea and Latter Part a SnowStorm . . . so Ends*

MONDAY 5TH *First Part strong gales from West with a SnowStorm a bad sea on. . . at 8 AM found our chain parted tried all we could to get in the chain, but being short handed we could not, had to unshackle and let it go it did not appear as if there was much chain hanging to the bows, saw a Bark made sail for him the bark for a while then made sail and went off, hulled to the W. ward Middle Part . . .got our cedge [sic] anchor on the bow and bent the chain unrove our chains from our forward Lantern and stowed them below wind N thick snowstorm north laid WNW*

TUESDAY 6TH *First Part a thick snowstorm wind North laid WNW at 4 PM a Smothering Snow-Storm Middle Part squally Latter Part a SnowStorm saw a Ship and Brig to windward set the Colors and fired the gun they paid no regard to us a thick snowstorm so Ends*

WEDNESDAY 7TH *thick SnowStorm blowing strong at 5 PM sounded got 35 fathoms at 1/2 past 1 sounded with 20 fathoms line got no bottom at 5 AM brought up on Montauk 1 1/2 Miles west of the Light house on a reef of Rocks came near drowning stove our boat all to pieces froze our fingers the Boat is near high and dry*

THE SECOND NANTUCKET LIGHTSHIP: No. 1—1855

The government moved with more expediency than normal to replace the lost No. 11 with one of a newer and more substantial type. Designed to be collision-proof, the new vessel, officially designated No. 1, was a solidly built 275-ton schooner, 103 feet long with a 24-foot beam and powered only by sail. Built at the Kittery Navy Yard in Maine of white oak and dense live oak from the swamps of Virginia, No. 1 endured calm and bitter weather, summer's heat and winter's cold as a good friend to mariners for over seventy-five years.

No. 1 served mariners for three quarters of a century, including 37 years on the Nantucket South Shoals station. Solidly built of oak, she endured storms strong enough to break her loose from her mooring at least 25 times.

A less placid image of No. 1 on station. The obvious limitations of photography in storm conditions force us to use our imaginations to picture the experience of the sea's rage aboard a lightship.

No. 1 was built with two hulls, with salt poured between them to "keep her sweet" and prevent rotting from rainwater seepage. The vessel had two 71-foot masts for sails and two 41-foot lantern masts stepped just forward of the sailing masts. Eight octagonal copper lanterns, each five feet wide by four feet high, made up each of the ship's two lights and showed a fixed white light. The lanterns could only be hoisted 25 feet above the deck, for when higher they made the small lightship top-heavy. A large fog bell swung ten feet forward of the forward deck and was kept tolling at two-minute intervals day and night when fog engulfed the ship.

This sturdy ship, first placed on station twenty-four miles out at sea from Sankaty Head Lighthouse,

housed in its tiny quarters a crew of ten men who cared for the two lights. The station was a busy place from the beginning; a letter from Captain Allen Gifford of the lightship states that "for the year ending January 27th, 1857, there passed that station, 124 ships, 218 barks, 271 brigs, 53 sloops, and 15 steamers; making a total of 815 vessels. Of this number 63 spoke and took their departure from the Light Ship, and 4 changed their course on the signal being set, 'You are standing into danger.'"

A brutal storm on October 13, 1878, tore Nantucket Lightship No. 1 from her mooring. She drifted helplessly south-southeast out to sea, unable to sail westerly in the storm. When the storm subsided, the lightship was 800 miles away, near the island of

The tall smokestack of a coal-burner marks lightship No. 66, built at Bath Iron Works at a cost of $70,000. She served on the Nantucket South Shoals station at the turn of the century. Note the added mast that served as an aerial for her pioneering Marconi "wireless telegraph"—a.k.a. ship-to-shore radio, installed in 1905. No. 66 straddles two worlds in this photograph: her radio mast stands above a light mast that seems ready to carry sail. Her stack contrasts sharply with the canvas sails of the sloop passing behind her.

Bermuda. The gale ended and, being truly hearty mariners, the crew made their way back to Nantucket under the lightship's own sail. Three months of repairs were needed, allowing the crew the luxury of Thanksgiving and Christmas dinners with their families—and then back to their isolated vigil on the Nantucket shoals.

The old No. 1 was set adrift more times than can be counted, always dutifully returning on her own to resume her watch on the Nantucket South Shoals station. In 1892 the station was moved ten miles farther offshore, exposing the lightship even more to the ravages of the Atlantic. No. 1 was taken off station and retired to a more protected location at this point, having spent thirty-seven years warning maritime traffic off the Nantucket Shoals. Her replacements, No. 9 and No. 39, were not well-suited for the rugged weather of the open Atlantic, and both were withdrawn after only a few months' service.

IN PURSUIT OF
A SEAWORTHY
NANTUCKET LIGHTSHIP

The government then built a new vessel of the "sea floor" type, officially called No. 54. She was almost lost in the first heavy gale, so No. 39 was put back on station, later to be replaced by No. 54 again. The government was obviously having difficulty developing a vessel to withstand the tumultuous storms that often battered the Nantucket South Shoals station.

A vessel was finally designed especially for the rough weather off Nantucket Island. They built the Nantucket No. 66 using a new and more seaworthy type of construction. In response to the increasing draft of commercial ships, the station was again moved farther out into the ocean, beyond Asia Rip in 180 feet of water some forty-two miles southeast of Nantucket Island. In 1896 No. 66 was stationed on the Nantucket South Shoals, remaining there for eleven years.

LIGHTSHIP DAYS
AND NIGHTS

For some forty years, up until 1894, a Nantucketer always captained the Nantucket South Shoals Light Vessel, and islanders were numerous among the crew. Some claim that all the crewmembers for the first ten or fifteen years were Nantucket-born. The Nantucket men commanding the lightship during those early years were Samuel Bunker, Allen Gifford, George C. Gardner II, Thomas James, Benjamin Morris, Andrew J. Sandsbury, Isaac Hamblin, and David E. Ray. Captain Sandsbury served the longest, spending five years as mate and later commanding the vessel for an additional nineteen years.

Many hours, weeks, and months spent aboard the lightship led to inevitable boredom and inspired the creation of the now famous Nantucket lightship

Nantucket lightship baskets have become a popular symbol of the island and of the men who spent long weeks and months aboard the lightships. Compact and requiring few tools, making these rattan baskets was a great way for crewmembers to pass the time profitably. This nest of seven baskets, fashioned by Captain James Wyer, earned a two-dollar prize for its maker from the Nantucket Agricultural Society in 1879.

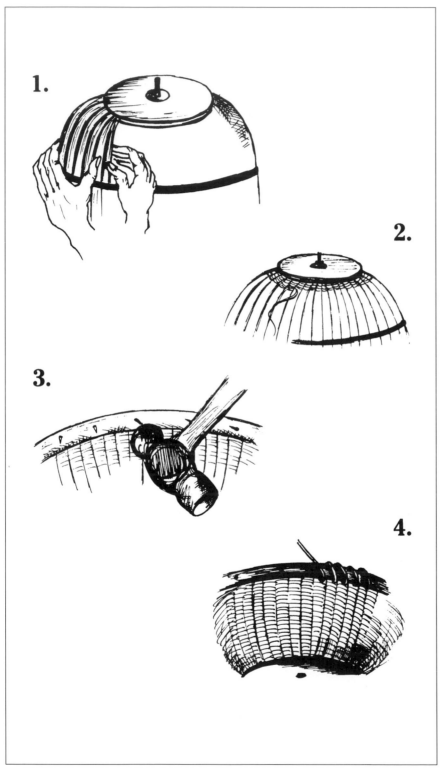

1.

2.

3.

4.

Making a Nantucket lightship basket.

baskets. The early lightship crews, who spent four months out of every six aboard ship, had ample time to weave the unusual baskets. Some men produced upwards of 200 of them, all as the little lightship bounced around in the Atlantic.

That Nantucket lightship baskets were light in weight and took up little space made them an ideal way to while away the time on the tiny lightship. Most of the crew chewed plug tobacco, and the tobacco boxes made ideal bottoms for the baskets. With flat wooden bases, the baskets were woven of rattan on wooden molds made of larger pieces of wood such as pieces of an old ship mast. Sometimes they were made in "nests" of five or eight sizes designed to fit perfectly inside one another. The baskets were brought ashore to be sold by family members to augment the crewman's income. Later, when the men left lightship duty, they brought the craft ashore, and the art of making lightship baskets became distinctively part of Nantucket. The art of making these exceptional baskets has continued for many generations.

As No. 66 was first taking her place on South Shoals station at the turn of the century, everything new in the world of science had piqued America's curiosity. Many people had heard about a gentleman in London named Guglielmo Marconi, famous for his work with wireless telegraphy.

Hearing about his wondrous ship-to-shore communications in England, the New York *Herald Tribune* invited him to New York to report on the America's Cup races for the paper. Marconi, a yachting enthusiast, agreed, and in 1899 he came to America to cover the event. After setting up both ship and shore aerials on poles 150 feet high, Marconi was ready to communicate by his wireless telegraphy the positions of the boats in the America's Cup race as they competed.

Lightship No. 71, built at Bath Iron Works in Maine, held the Nantucket South Shoals station for a few months in early 1906. In 1918, having broadcast a message to passing ships that a German submarine was nearby, she was sunk by gunfire from the sub. Fortunately, the crew had been allowed to abandon ship before the firing began.

The first Marconi radio tower on Bunker Hill in 'Sconset, c. 1902. The three-part mast is clearly visible.

fared better than the two famous sailboats, for he sent messages by wireless to his land station in Fort Hancock, New Jersey. They, in turn, telegraphed the newspaper, which ran the headline, "NO RACE." The tension that mounted during several more days of delay due to uncooperative weather generated enthusiasm for Marconi's wireless telegraphy all over the country. At long last the races took place, with *Columbia* the eventual victor. Marconi sent a total of twelve hundred messages during the event and in the process became a global hero and in 1909 he shared the Nobel Prize in Physics.

From Marconi's successful coverage of the America's Cup by wireless, it became evident that wireless telegraphy could be an invaluable safeguard to mariners. A major advance in ship-to-shore communication took place on Nantucket during the summer of 1901.

In a joint venture, the *Herald Tribune* and Marconi set up a wireless station in Siasconset manned by Marconi's technicians. Participation in this communications breakthrough offered the *Herald Tribune* the

On the scheduled day of the first race, the two yachting challengers stood ready at the starting line to continue a rivalry that had begun forty-eight years earlier. But the *Shamrock* of Sir Thomas Lipton and the *Columbia* of C. Oliver Iselin were not to have a race that first day, for there was virtually no wind. Marconi

Raising the flag to open the Marconi station at 'Sconset in 1901. Miss Margaret Fawcett does the honors.

The Marconi Wireless Telegraph Company's permanent station in 'Sconset. The house still stands.(Inset left) Harry Holden, one of Marconi's original operators on Nantucket. Marconi wanted him in New York, but love prevailed. Holden stayed on Nantucket, where he married Maria Folger (inset right).

opportunity to score a journalistic coup, reporting the whereabouts of transatlantic vessels in the newspaper several days in advance of their arrival. With the government's permission, preparations were made to install wireless telegraph equipment on the Nantucket South Shoals Lightship No. 66.

In order for the telegraph to work effectively, the operators located the highest southeasterly land on Nantucket. The area, known as Bunker Hill, lies south of Milestone Road just before one enters the hamlet of 'Sconset. There the island's first wireless station was built.

On the "summit" of Bunker Hill a lofty aerial mast measuring 170 feet from ground to truck was installed. It consisted of "three parts—a lower mast, top-mast and top-gallant mast," just like those of a sailing ship. Just getting the mammoth spars to 'Sconset turned out to be a monumental task.

The masts for both the shore station and the lightship were built in New Bedford, Massachusetts. It was claimed by some of the oldest seafaring inhabitants of the ancient whaling port that the wireless "sticks" were the largest ever shaped in New Bedford, where many a fine tall ship had been built. Made of Oregon pine, the mainmast alone was seventy-seven and a half feet in length, eighteen inches in diameter, and weighed three and a half tons without rigging.

To everyone's chagrin, the steamship that sailed across Nantucket Sound from the mainland to the islands flatly refused to carry the masts because of their bulky character. A quaint Nantucket steamer, half wrecker and half fishing boat, was chartered to tow the spars the seventy miles across Nantucket Sound from New Bedford.

At the same time a topmast, sprit, and spare topmast, together with all the necessary gear and wireless equipment to be installed on the Nantucket Lightship, were sent to Woods Hole on Cape Cod. From there, a lightship tender transported the gear to the Nantucket South Shoals Lightship so the work of installing the equipment could be done while the shore station was being prepared. The topmast was mounted on the lightship as it lay anchored on station forty-two miles out in the Atlantic Ocean—no simple feat.

It took nine days of preparation, filled with frustration and delay, to bring about the first ship-to-shore transmission. Finally, at ten o'clock on the morning of August 12, 1901, on Nantucket South Shoals Lightship No. 66 the practical application of wireless telegraphy for ship-to-shore communication was first demonstrated. A message was transmitted from 'Sconset: "Signal clear; am using plain aerial. Good luck."

Soon after that, fifty-two miles from the lightship, the incoming ocean liner *Lucania* sent the Nantucket Lightship a message, which was relayed to the 'Sconset wireless station and then forwarded by telegraph cable to New York City. Clumsy as it now seems, this multistage system, operating entirely in Morse code, made communications history. As a result of this success, No. 66 became the first lightship in the United

Proudly flying the pennant of the Lighthouse Service, the tender Azalea *is shown here some time after 1912.*

States with permanent radio facilities, an extraordinary breakthrough in maritime safety.

The original wireless station at 'Sconset was completely taken over by Marconi Wireless in 1904, only to be destroyed by a fire in the electrical equipment on November 15, 1907. It is of interest to note that a young man named David Sarnoff was one of Marconi's two wireless operators on Nantucket. Marconi wanted both men to go to his New York station, but Sarnoff's

partner Harry Holden had fallen in love with a local woman, Maria Folger, and he remained on Nantucket to marry her. Sarnoff, however, followed his destiny to New York, where he became world renowned as the founder of the Radio Corporation of America, or RCA.

The original Marconi wireless operation then moved to a small house (which still stands) not far away on Main Street in 'Sconset, remaining there until 1922. A plaque in the front yard of the home reads: "1st Wireless Telegraph Station in U.S. to communicate with ships at sea - Marconi system installed here by NY Herald Tribune in 1901 and 1st message from ocean liner "Lucania" via South Shoals lightship August 15, 1901."

It continues: "This Siasconset Station received call for help 'CQD' from S.S. *Republic* in collision with steamship *Florida*: January 23, 1909."

On that date the White Star Line's *Republic*, heading for Europe, was struck by the Italian liner *Florida* in a thick fog. The *Republic* flashed the international distress signal "CQD" in Morse code, and the

Nantucket Lightship picked up the signal and quickly sent messages to ships in the area to help the stricken vessels. The steamship *Baltic* came to their aid, rescuing 1650 people from both vessels, miraculously without loss of life. The event marked a major advance and affirmed the practicality of wireless communication at sea.

That same year, the crew of the Nantucket South Shoals Lightship were saved from going down with their own ship, No. 58, when they discovered that she was taking on water and sent out a distress call. The tender *Azalea* responded. As the *Azalea* was towing her

Nantucket Lightship No. 106 on station in 1930.

No. 85, the Nantucket Shoals Light Vessel from 1907 to 1923. On October 18, 1917, a German U-Boat torpedoed five merchant ships in the area of the lightship. Their crews, numbering 115 men in total, were able to reach the lightship via lifeboats, the submarine captain having allowed them to escape. There the grateful sailors took refuge, their fourteen lifeboats tied in a string behind the lightship. No lives were lost in the episode.

to shore, the lightship suddenly sank into the depths of the dark and hostile Atlantic Ocean. The men were grateful for the radio; without it, they might not have escaped with their lives.

Until 1864, sperm oil had illuminated the lights of the Nantucket Lightship. After that date, lard, half the price of sperm oil, and later kerosene, served as fuel until the lights were electrified in 1906. The electric incandescent light completely revolutionized lightship duty. The crew merely had to switch the light on or off twice a day and occasionally change a light bulb. No longer did they need to clean reflectors, trim wicks, and polish glass.

In 1907, lightship No. 85 was placed on duty, to remain on the Nantucket South Shoals for sixteen years. In 1911 the Nantucket Lightship added a submarine bell, whose function was based on the principal that sound travels faster under water than in air. In bad weather the lightship would simultaneously sound the fog

LIGHTSHIP DUTY RECALLED

Lighthouse historian Ken Black's thirty-two years in the Coast Guard included considerable lightship duty. He considers lightships to be the most neglected area of America's maritime history, and his own recollections provide an interesting glimpse of life at the Nantucket South Shoals station:

In the post-World War II years it was commonly known that newly appointed Coast Guard Warrant Boatswains could expect to be assigned to a lightship. Much to my surprise, however, my initial assignment was to a lifeboat station instead of one of the "Red Raiders." My joy was short-lived, as in March 1956 I received orders for the WAL-536, Relief, *at Boston.*

The WAL-536 was a relatively new lightship, having been built in 1931. Her displacement was 630 tons. She was 133 feet long with a 30 foot beam. She was diesel electric, with four relatively small engines driving generators. This arrangement was an engineer's delight. The engine room was spacious and well laid out. The last few lightships built by the Coast Guard had basically the same engine arrangement.

The steering arrangement, on the other hand, left much to be desired. It was totally hand powered. That, coupled with low horsepower, made maneuvering the ship very interesting. Any engine orders had to be carefully watched, and full power was never ordered without ordering the helmsman to secure the wheel so that it would not be torn out of his hands.

Life aboard the ship on station was usually great. There was a regular watch-standing routine for most of the crew. One third were ashore at all times. Although there was no television reception on the Nantucket Station at that time, the Relief, *being based in Boston, had access to the Navy film program. We supplied the naval staff with plenty of coffee when our ship was in port, and in return we would sail with about fifty recent movies.*

continued on page 117

The doomed No. 117 on station at Nantucket South Shoals.

horn and the submarine bell. The approaching ship would calculate the difference in seconds that they had received the two signals and divide that number by 5.5, which would give them the distance between their ship and the lightship in nautical miles. On August 23, 1923, No. 85 was replaced by Nantucket Lightship No. 106, which began its eight years of service.

In the spring of 1934, the crew of the lightship on station at the time—No. 117—had a frightening experience. Despite the submarine bell and all the other warning systems used by the lightship, the passenger liner *Washington* sideswiped her, shearing off a

lifeboat, boat davits, and an antenna. The liner and its passengers escaped unharmed.

Tragically, the incident was only an eerie premonition of the event of May 15 of that year, when the White Star Line's mammoth *Olympic* made the lightship crew's worst nightmare come true. The 46,000-ton British liner, sister ship of the ill-fated *Titanic,* was traveling at sixteen knots in dense fog when it crashed into the diminutive lightship, splitting her in half and sinking her instantly. (One of the *Olympic*'s more insensitive officers was overheard to remark that "It was a crack shot; we hit her right on the 'U'"—the middle letter of the name NANTUCKET painted on the lightship's side.) Four members of the eleven-man crew went down with the ship, and three died later from injuries. The four remaining men were miraculously saved. The true cause of the collision is unknown; but an investigation by marine experts concluded that atmospheric conditions, primarily fog, distorted perceptions of the lightship's foghorn and the *Olympic*'s penetrating deep-throated whistle.

The White Star Line, absorbed later that year by Cunard, paid $500,000 in damages to build a larger and stronger replacement lightship and to compensate the families of the lost crew. The replacement, No. 112, cost $350,000 and was built in 1936 by Pusey & Jones of Wilmington, Delaware.

From its launching in 1936 until 1942, the Nantucket No. 112 remained on station. Only in World War II was she withdrawn and replaced by a buoy, as lightships were rightly regarded as easy targets for enemy submarines.

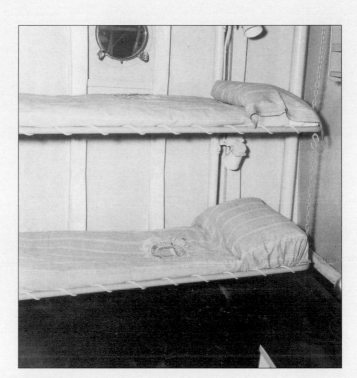

The port forward "stateroom" on lightship WAL-612.

I relieved Nantucket Station three times. Only one was for routine reasons. One of the others was when it was discovered that she had an overhand knot in her anchor chain. A tender had to assist and actually cut the chain. To date no one has been able to come up with a plausible explanation for the knot. This is a matter of record as having occurred three times in the lightship service, twice to the Nantucket Lightship.

`The other time we relieved Nantucket was due to sickness on board. The whole crew came down with a flu-type illness, so I was ordered to proceed and relieve her for a short period, which turned out to be 63 days. We proceeded well seaward of Cape Cod to avoid the Cape Cod Canal tidal problems. Late in the evening when we were about ten miles away from Nantucket Station, I found a can buoy adrift and reported it to the Coast Guard District, noting that I could sink it with rifle fire. The

continued on page 119

Beginning work on Nantucket Light Vessel No. 117 in 1929.

During the war, No. 112 was painted gray and positioned at the entrance to the harbor at Portland, Maine to prevent German submarines from entering. After the War, No. 112 was reclassified as WAL-534. From 1958 to 1960 WAL-534, later converted from steam to diesel, often served as a relief ship on the Nantucket Station. After 1972 her successor *Nantucket II*, built in 1952 to be the Ambrose Lightship off New York Harbor, rotated with WAL-534 on the Nantucket South Shoals station.

With her double hull, the Nantucket WAL-534, or No. 112 as she is still better known, represented a

pinnacle of lightship design. In 1936 she was the largest lightship ever built, 149 feet long and displacing 915 tons, and she was designed specifically to withstand the extremes of the Nantucket South Shoals station. After the *Olympic* disaster, the goal also was to create a lightship that would be the most indestructible ever built. If the outer hull is breached, an inner hull remains, and in a collision the crew would have a very good chance of survival unless the ship was cut completely in half. No. 112 has more escape hatches than any other lightship, affording the crew numerous ways to abandon ship; this feature was a response to several other lightship tragedies in which vessels were lost with all hands trapped below deck.

Lightships were not designed to be under way at sea but to take a pounding while anchored. The bridge windows of No. 112 are very small, for they are subjected to heavy seas; the bow is blunt to meet waves. Since visibility is poor from the bridge, the helmsman would steer from a flying bridge topside when the vessel was under way. It has the feeling of piloting an old tall ship with its high masts. The engine is not controlled from the bridge, but by a system of bells that ring in the engine room, signaling the engineer to adjust the engine.

The living quarters on the Nantucket Lightship were Spartan, with only senior officers having their own cabin. Diesel generators ran constantly, filling the air with a low, monotonous din. Even on the calmest day on the Nantucket Station, with only ground swells to contend with, the little lightship would dip and roll

District came back with orders to attempt to recover the buoy. By then it was fully dark, although relatively calm. After much maneuvering, we were able to recover the buoy with our anchor davit and windlass. We were probably the first red *buoy tender.*

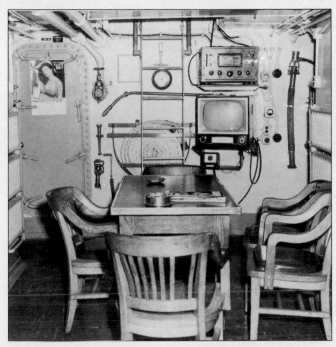

An "entertainment center" aboard No. 112 in 1958. Television made lightship duty significantly more bearable.

Lightships are placed in harm's way! This is no light statement. Almost every lightship was struck by passing vessels. With the advent of radio direction finders, the mariner homed in on the lightships, of which the classic example occurred when the liner Olympic *struck the Nantucket Lightship right amidships, sinking her with a loss of seven crew. Any time a vessel approached close to a lightship, its propeller beats could be heard clearly below decks. When we heard propellers, everyone automatically came topside, and on some occasions the general alarm was sounded.*

continued on page 121

No. 112 under construction at Pusey & Jones in Wilmington, Delaware on March 21, 1936. When launched, she was the largest lightship that had ever been built in the United States.

constantly. Floating in thirty fathoms near the dreaded quicksand shallows of the South Shoals, No. 112 was held stationary by a 3 1/2-ton anchor attached to 150 fathoms of chain strong enough to withstand 100-knot gales. Unlike their predecessors, latter-day crews were on station for only three weeks at a stretch, and they received extra leave to compensate for their isolated duty.

Many of the fittings for this diminutive lightship were a cross between those of much larger steamships and the old tall ships. The small lightship had a huge ship's bell of a size usually found on a bigger vessel and extra large ventilators that seem exaggerated in proportion to its size. She is fastened by extra-large rivets large enough to hold an ocean-going tugboat together.

The last decades of the Nantucket South Shoals Lightship were eventful ones. The lightship continued to be a relevant aid to navigation into the 1970s, conveying weather information and helping in rescue missions. The Nantucket lightship (WAL-536, the *Relief*, at the time), for example, served as an important communications link in the aftermath of the collision in heavy fog between the Italian liner *Andrea Doria* and the smaller *Stockholm* in 1956. Although the *Andrea Doria* sank, the immediate response of the French liner *Ile de France* and quick work by the *Stockholm*'s crew prevented the incident from becoming a major tragedy. The lightship served the same function in 1976, when the tanker *Argo Merchant* ran aground on the shoals, spilling millions of gallons of oil.

The lightship endured her share of batterings as well. In October of 1954 Hurricane Edna pummeled No. 112 unmercifully as she stayed on her post. The lightship's Coast Guard crew battled seventy-foot seas and winds of up to 110 miles per hour. One mountainous wave hit the small vessel squarely, snapping the anchor chain, smashing five glass

The Relief *was on Nantucket Station when the* Andrea Doria–Stockholm *collision occurred. It was thick fog, and the liner* Ile de France, *rushing to the scene at full speed, passed close to the lightship. Needless to say, the crew were all topside, nervously watching its approach on radar and then having to crane their necks upward to see the name on the bow of the liner.*

Life aboard lightships on station can also be dull, boring, busy, and at times terrifying. Probably the most annoying thing is when visibility is reduced to the point that it is necessary to start the fog signal. Sometimes this lasts for days. When speaking to someone you simply stop talking when the fog horn starts and resume when it stops. The galley on many of the lightships is under the fog horn mount, so of course fog is dreaded by the cook. When watching movies during fog, we learned to read lips on the screen fairly well.

Feeding the crew during heavy weather was a real problem for the cook. Even with fiddles [small fences that hold dishes in place on a table] *and wet dishcloths, it was impossible to use the mess tables. We mainly ate stews and foods that could be eaten out of a bowl. You just put your arm around a stanchion and ate hanging on.*

I will never forget my first three-day Nor'easter on Nantucket Station. I stayed awake the first couple of nights, thinking that if any problems developed they would come at night. The flesh gets weak, so on the third night I turned in, leaving orders to call me when there was enough daylight to see. The watch called me, and as I started up the ladder to the bridge, I felt her dig into a big sea. After it passed I went up and saw that she simply shook off the sea with no problem. I never stayed up another night because of sea conditions after that.

I have said many times that lightship duty was the best duty I had in all my years in the Coast Guard.

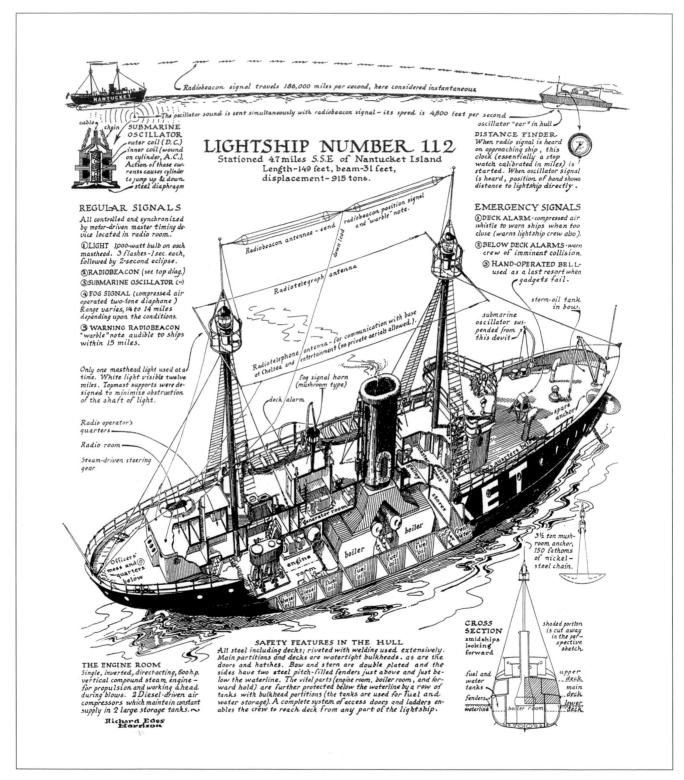

Cut-away view of Nantucket Lightship No. 112, detailing the operation of all the ship's signaling devices as well as the many safety features built into new lightships in the aftermath of the Olympic *tragedy.*

Tending a lightship's machinery was a never-ending job.

portholes, destroying the wheel and all instruments in the wheelhouse, and sweeping the instruments from the flying bridge. The courageous crew improvised a spare mushroom anchor, but the ship had already drifted ten miles toward the dangerous Nantucket shoals.

A second huge wave following close behind the first threw the port engine ventilator to the starboard side of the lightship, where it became wedged under a lifeboat as water poured down the stack. The same wave also bent the ship's rudder. Water streamed into the vessel through a jagged hole in the bow, and fires broke out below. The electrical system failed completely, as did the foghorn.

With the lifeboats also smashed to pieces, there was no possibility of abandoning ship. The only hope

The engine room of No. 112, featuring the huge diesel-driven generators that powered her lights and other equipment.

was to send an SOS. The radioman, painfully burned by sparks erupting from the ship's radio, heroically sent off only one message: "We're taking a helluva beating."

The fast response of two Coast Guard cutters, a reconnaissance plane, and the buoy tender *Hornbeam* from Woods Hole saved the lightship crew, who had truly expected to die. Along with the other damage, the extreme force of the wind had pushed the deckhouse back a full foot.

In 1959 another hurricane drove the lightship from her moorings, pushing her eighty miles from her station as she dragged her two enormous anchors. For several days, with her radio out of commission, the helpless lightship was thought lost. In the end, however, the sturdy vessel survived this tempest as well.

The lightship crew even got to play its part in international relations. One story is told of a Russian trawler in the 1960s coming closer and closer to the Nantucket Lightship. The captain of the lightship warned him not to come so close. Shortly thereafter, the Russian trawler came too close again, and the captain of the lightship took a flare-gun and shot it into the pilot house of the Russian vessel, risking an international incident. Having learned discretion, however, the Russian trawler chose to keep his distance.

As the use of Loran and satellite navigation for tracking vessels became more widespread in the 1970s, annual expenditures of hundreds of thousands of dollars to keep a lightship on station were regarded as excessive. The Coast Guard determined that unmanned aids to navigation could be equally effective, and so an automated buoy, cheaper and subject to less human risk than the lightship, replaced the historic Nantucket Lightship in 1978.

Today a mammoth forty-foot buoy with high-technology communication equipment, long-range automatic lights, and sound-in-air devices floats in its place, some fifty miles south-southeast of Sankaty Head in the middle of the main north-south Atlantic shipping channel. Having none of the charisma of the Nantucket Lightship, the buoy functions more like a traffic signal on a superhighway.

Lightships represent, in a romantic and metaphysical way, the best of two worlds. Like lighthouses, they are symbols of guidance, of the light at the end of the tunnel, of salvation; but as ocean-going vessels

Five of these portholes on the bridge of No. 112 were blown in by a wave during Hurricane Edna in 1954. The wheel and the bridge instruments were destroyed at the same time.

Lightship No. 112 on station at some point after 1965; by this time her stack had been lowered after her conversion to diesel power. Her lanterns, fog horn, and radio antennas are clearly visible.

they also conjure up the images of tall ships sailing over the bounding sea and valiant seamen battling great storms. It is no wonder that No. 112, retired from duty but still a living, fully operational ship, continues to endear herself to crowds wherever she goes. Still proudly wearing the name NANTUCKET in bright white letters on her red hull, No. 112 is now based at the Intrepid Museum in New York City. With a volunteer crew, each year she becomes a traveling exhibit that moves from seaport to seaport along the East Coast. While they win friends for the vessel, the voyages of No. 112 have the added value of motivating her crew to keep her engines running and the ship fully operational.

There is no doubt that the crews of the Nantucket South Shoals Lightship displayed a quality of heroism that touches both our hearts and our imaginations. Merely to have served on the Nantucket Station, more exposed to the rigors of the ocean than any other in the world, was a feat in itself. Nantucket lightship duty required a stamina that was not only physical but mental and moral; only the long and dangerous voyages of the old-time Nantucket whaling vessels required comparable endurance.

Nantucket I, *the last lightship on the Nantucket South Shoals station. Our story cannot close "with the traditional look to the future of lightships," wrote historian Willard Flint, "for there is none." Their story, however, constitutes "a unique and proud section of America's maritime heritage."*

Flying the flag signal "Peter Charlie," meaning "light vessel off-station," Nantucket Lightship No. 112 makes for port. Note the high stack of her coal-burning (before 1965) years.

Over time, 120 lightships had been placed in service in the navigable waters of the United States. The Nantucket Lightship was the very last of those heroic vessels to see duty. In its final radio transmission to Coast Guard headquarters in Washington, the crew of the Nantucket South Shoals Lightship sent this epitaph for their service:

Nantucket...*was the last lightship in the Coast Guard and last of the Nantucket Shoals lightships that have watched over that area since June 1854.... An important chapter of Coast Guard history ended today. We must now look elsewhere to find the stuff that sea stories are made of.*

NANTUCKET LIGHTS: WHAT OF THEIR FUTURE?

What's past is prologue.

—*Shakespeare,*

The Tempest, Act II, *Scene* i

Sankaty Head Lighthouse teeters on an eroding precipice; Great Point light attracts vandals almost as often as sightseers; the eelgrass on the hillocks surrounding Brant Point Lighthouse is trampled flat. We might well fear for the future of Nantucket's lighthouses. These stalwart sentinels of the shoreline have no way to defend themselves against time or apathy, and so they must depend for their survival on our appreciation of their history and on our sense of place.

The challenges they pose and the questions they ask are many. Do we move them when they are in jeopardy, or do we let nature take its course? What relevance do these structures have for us today, when their functions can be assumed by gadgets that are more reliable and more effective? What is the best way to remember and honor the services these beacons rendered to the seafaring island of Nantucket?

Gone are the great whaling ships and busy warehouses of Nantucket Town. Gone, too, are the flotillas of cargo schooners that once paraded up and down Nantucket Sound, forming a vital lifeline between the ports of America's northeast coast. Gone are the great luxury liners that slid southward of the island, their presence noted only by the radio operators of the lightships they passed. Gone is the fleet of catboats that once swept across

129

Nantucket Harbor, dredging for scallops. The townspeople of Nantucket have preserved the integrity of their antique village; the island's museums proudly display bits and pieces of Nantucket's maritime history. But what remains of the *real* past?

Alone among the remnants of nautical Nantucket, the surviving lighthouses and lightships give us an authentic glimpse of life on the old island when it was sustained by fishing and whaling. They alone are situated in their original locations, where sights and sounds and smells allow us to share the experience of those who built and tended them. A clear, sunny day at Brant Point, a gathering storm off Sankaty Head, an icy winter wind scouring Great Point, and even the cramped sweat-and-paint smell of a lightship cabin can bring maritime Nantucket to life in ways no postcard or scrimshaw-filled glass cabinet can. These lights enable us to *live* the island's seafaring past.

Now it is left for us to respond to the challenges. What course will we choose? Nantucket's lights can still guide us, this time backward in time toward a better understanding of who we are and where we came from. Even as they faithfully continue to guide mariners toward safe harbor, they serve as icons to remind us of the human values they symbolize.

As long as they shine, in memory and in fact, the lighthouses and lightships of Nantucket will speak to us of the courage, humility, and integrity of those who built and kept them. Today the same commitment is asked of those who would remember and preserve the heritage of the island's legendary beacons. For Nantucket without its history would be, to paraphrase Melville, nothing more than "beach, without a background."

Acknowledgments

I t occurred to me a few years ago that if they could speak, each of Nantucket's beacons would tell a unique and colorful story. I had always loved photographing all the lighthouses on the island, and I was further inspired after taking a seminar on architectural photography at the University of Florida's Preservation Institute: Nantucket.

Nantucket Lights began when Maurice Gibbs, now president of the Nantucket Life Saving Museum, was suggested to me as someone who might help me find people who had lived at Nantucket lighthouses and served on the Nantucket Lightship. At my first meeting with Maurice, I was also introduced to the late Bob Caldwell, the Life Saving Museum's founder and guiding spirit. Maurice and Bob enthusiastically shared recollections and insights that furthered my understanding of Nantucket's maritime past. They also directed me to people with personal experience at Great Point, Sankaty Head, and Brant Point lighthouses and the Nantucket South Shoals Light Vessels.

I really don't feel as though I have personally written this book. Rather, it has been written for me in the lives of the many wonderful people who over time have lived in the lighthouses and on the Nantucket Lightship. I am but a collector who happened along and assembled the many pieces scattered among archives and in libraries, homespun photo albums, and in the hearts of Nantucketers young and old.

To all of those who generously took the time to share with me their lives and their boundless love of Nantucket, I extend my heartfelt thanks. Without their assistance and support this book would never have become a reality. Those who lent me photographs and other memorabilia, not really knowing me, showed a trust that I see as the very essence of Nantucket's island community.

After a while this book took on an uncanny quality of its own. I was waiting for rejection on some level; for someone, somewhere, to refuse to share their knowledge of Nantucket's lighthouses and the Nantucket Lightship. It truly never happened. Instead, each door that opened led to another door that opened on equally valuable material, and *Nantucket Lights* just seemed to gather more momentum.

Special tribute is due to Ethel Larsen Hamilton, who went to great lengths to organize all the information she had about Sankaty Head and the other lighthouses as well as about the Nantucket Lightship. I consider her my best cheerleader, sending me little notes year round and collecting material for me. Her enthusiasm was wonderful and greatly appreciated. Bill Grieder, Jeannette Haskins Killen, Reggie Reed, and Vic Reed are the children of some of Nantucket's finest lightkeepers (as is Ethel Larsen Hamilton). Their willingness to share childhood memories was invaluable. So also was the help of Dan Kelliher and former lightship crewman Dick Mack, who both served with Nantucket's "Dirty Dozen," as those lightship enthusiasts affectionately called themselves, and of Chief Warrant Officer George Bassett, U.S.C.G (Ret.), who gave Great Point light a "tuxedo" of a restoration before its collapse.

My husband Tony Cahill has been a source of continuous and steadfast help with this book, patiently listening to my ideas, enabling me to pursue my research, and, most important, serving as my Sherlock Holmes. His probing questions clarified my thoughts and cast a bright light of their own on the subject of this book.

Others, too, deserve my deep gratitude. My mother and father, although they will never see this book, graciously instilled in me an adventurous and creative spirit and a desire to live and experience life fully. Albert "Bud" Egan encouraged me to continue with *Nantucket Lights* and gave me the opportunity to publish it through Mill Hill Press, and editor Peter Gow served as a thoughtful and dedicated guiding light for the endeavor. On and off Nantucket, others have assisted and guided me as well: Mimi Beman; Chief Warrant Officer Ken Black, U.S.C.G (Ret.); Dr. Robert Browning; Jean Cavelos; Helen Winslow Chase; James Claflin; Grace Coffin; Robert Dennis; Officer-in-Charge Jack Downey of Brant Point Coast Guard Station; Ruth Grieder; Jacqueline Haring; Robert Kaplan; Mike Kaylan; Kathy Knight; Jane Lamb; Reggie Levine; Peter MacGlashan; Charlotte Maison and her staff at the Nantucket Atheneum; Gayl Michael; Robert Mooney; Paul Morris; Elizabeth Oldham; Manuel Oliveira; Nat Philbrick; Arthur Railton; Jerry Roberts; Susan Ruddick; Renny Stackpole; Diane and Fred Swartz; Betsy Tyler; Jack Weinhold; Mary Woodruff; and the many artists and photographers whose creative endeavors are included in *Nantucket Lights*.

I am also indebted to the staffs of the following libraries and museums for the great assistance they rendered in my research for this book: the Boston Athenaeum; the Boston Public Library; the G.W. Blunt White Library at Mystic Seaport; the Intrepid Sea-Air-Space Museum; the Massachusetts Historical Society; the Edouard A. Stackpole Library and Research Center at the Nantucket Historical Association; the Nantucket Life Saving Museum; the National Archives; the New Bedford Free Public Library; the New York Public Library; the Old Dartmouth Historical Society Whaling Museum (New Bedford); the Peabody Essex Museum; the Rye Free Reading Room; the Shore Village Museum; the South Street Seaport Library; and the United States Coast Guard Archives.

Last but by no means least, I want to thank God for leading me on this journey on beautiful Nantucket Island.

Bibliography

Adamson, Hans Christian. *Keeper of the Lights.* New York, 1955.

Babcock, Edwina Stanton. *Nantucket Windows.* Nantucket, 1924.

Baker, Louise S. *Eunice Hussey.* Nantucket, 1938.

————. *By The Sea.* Nantucket, 1893.

Bliss, William Root. *Quaint Nantucket.* Cambridge, Massachusetts, 1896.

Byers, Edward. *The Nation of Nantucket.* Boston, 1987.

Carse, Robert. *Keeper of the Lights; A History of American Lighthouses.* New York, 1969.

Chamberlain, Barbara Blau. *These Fragile Outposts: A Geological Look at Cape Cod, Martha's Vineyard, and Nantucket.* Garden City, New York, 1964.

Coe, Douglas. *Marconi, Pioneer of Radio.* New York, 1943.

Davis, Merrill R. and Gilman, William H. *The Letters of Herman Melville.* New Haven, Connecticut, 1960.

Douglas-Lithgow, R.A. *Nantucket: A History.* New York, 1914.

Flint, Willard. *Lightships and Lightship Stations of the U.S. Government.* Washington, 1989.

Folger, Eva C.G. *The Glacier's Gift.* New Haven, Connecticut, 1911.

Gardner, Arthur H. *Wrecks Around Nantucket, Since the Settlement of the Island, and the Incidents Connected Therewith, Embracing Over Seven Hundred Vessels.* New Bedford, Massachusetts, 1915.

Godfrey, Edward K. *The Island of Nantucket—What It Was and What It Is.* Boston, 1882.

Gleason, Sarah C. *Kindly Lights: A History of the Lighthouses of Southern New England.* Boston, 1991.

Hart, Joseph C. *Miriam Coffin, or The Whale-Fisherman.* New York, 1834; Mill Hill Press edition, 1995.

Holland, Francis Ross Jr. *America's Lighthouses.* New York, 1972.

Kobbe, Gustav. "Life on the South Shoal Lightship." *Century Magazine,* August 18, 1891.

Kynett, Harold H. *Unforgettable Intimacies.* Privately published, 1965.

Labaree, Leonard, ed. *The Papers of Benjamin Franklin," Volume I (1706-1734).* New Haven, Connecticut, 1959.

Lacouture, Captain James. "Early Aviation on Nantucket." *Historic Nantucket,* Spring 1992.

Lamb, Jane. *Wauwinet.* Privately published, 1990.

Mackay, Dick. *Nantucket, Nantucket, Nantucket!* Siasconset, Massachusetts, 1981.

Macy, Obed. *The History of Nantucket.* Boston, 1835; reprinted Nantucket, 1970.

Macy, William F. *The Nantucket Scrap Basket, Being A Collection of Characteristic Stories and Sayings of the People of the Town and Island of Nantucket, Massachusetts.* Cambridge, Massachusetts, 1984.

Melville, Herman. *Moby-Dick, or The Whale.* New York, 1851; Random House edition, 1930.

Mooney, Robert F. *Tales of Nantucket.* Nantucket, 1990.

———— and Sigourney, André R. *The Nantucket Way.* Garden City, New York, 1980.

Morris, Paul C. and Morin, Joseph F. *The Island Steamers.* Nantucket, 1977.

Orleans Historical Society. *Rescue CG 36500.* Orleans, Massachusetts, 1985.

Philbrick, Nathaniel. *Away Off Shore.* Nantucket, 1994.

————. "Every Wave Is a Fortune: Nantucket Island and the Making of an American Icon." *The New England Quarterly*, September 1993.

Plowden, David, with text by Coffin, Patricia. *Nantucket*. New York, 1971.

Putnam, George R. *Lighthouses and Lightships of the United States*. Boston, 1933.

Robinson, John H. *Guide To Nantucket*. Nantucket, 1948.

Rust, Fred Winslow. *My Nantucket Out At Sea*. Privately published, 1944.

St. John de Crèvecoeur, J. Hector. *Letters From An American Farmer*. London, 1782; reprinted New York, 1904.

Seeler, Katherine and Edgar. *Nantucket Lightship Baskets*. Nantucket, 1972.

Sibley, Frank P. "That 'Delightful Tribe,' the Lighthouse Keepers." *Boston Globe*, July 7, 1929.

Snow, Edward Rowe. *Famous New England Lighthouses*. Boston, 1945.

————. *Storms and Shipwrecks of New England*. Boston, 1943.

Stackpole, Edouard A. *Life Saving, Nantucket*. Nantucket, 1972.

————. *The Forgotten Man of the Boston Tea Party* (pamphlet). Nantucket, 1973.

————. *The Sea-Hunters*. New York, 1953.

Stanton, Marianne Giffin, ed. *Nantucket Argument Settlers: A Complete History of Nantucket in Condensed Form*. Nantucket, 1994.

Stevenson, D. Alan. *The World's Lighthouses Before 1820*. London, 1959.

Thompson, Frederic L. *The Lightships of Cape Cod*. Portland, Maine, 1983.

Thoreau, Henry David. *Cape Cod*. Orleans, Massachusetts, 1984.

Turner, H.B. "The Nantucket South Shoals Station and the Vessels That Have Guarded It From 1854 to 1931." *Nantucket Inquirer and Mirror*, May 16, 1931.

United States Department of Commerce. *Lighthouse Service Bulletin*, Volume V, number 39. Washington, March 1939.

Updike, Richard W. "Augustin Fresnel and His Lighthouse Lenses." *American Neptune*, 1967.

————. "Winslow Lewis and the Lighthouses." *American Neptune*, 1968.

Whitney, Dudley. *The Lighthouse*. New York, 1989.

Whitten, Paul F. *Adventures on Nantucket Island For Young & Old*. Nantucket, 1960.

Williams, Winston. *Nantucket Then and Now*. New York, 1977.

Willoughby, Malcolm F. *Lighthouses of New England*. Boston, 1929.

Instructions to Lighthouse Keepers and Masters of Lighthouse Vessels, 1902; reprinted by the Great Lakes Lighthouse Keepers Association, 1989.

"Nantucket Lightships' Adventures Related." *Boston Traveler*, April 3, 1936.

Index

MARINE JOURNAL.
PORT OF NANTUCKET.

Monday, Jan 28th.
ARRIVED.
Steamer Telegraph, New Bedford.
Tuesday, Jan 29th
SAILED.
Steamer Telegraph, N. Bedford

MEMORANDA.

Ard at Mattapoisett Jan 27, brig Annawan, Taber, South Atlantic Ocean, with full cargo, 550 bbls sp oil. Spoke Oct 29, lat 16 50 S, lon 36 10 W, barks Dove, Forsyth, NL, clean, for Indian Ocean; Nov 3, lat 17 50 lon 36 50, Chase, Ricketson, NB, 100 sp on board, for California; 16th, lat 16 26 lon 36 10, Rainbow, of and fm Baltimore for Rio Janeiro; 20th, lat 16 58 lon 36 20, Mattapoisett, Wing, West-port, 230 sp; 22d, lat 17 20, lon 36 10, ship Susan, Howland, NB, clean, Capt sick; Dec 4, lat 17 25, lon 36 40, sch R C White, 31 ds fm Baltimore for San Francisco; 5th, lat 17 53 lon 36 56, brig Zoro-aster, Handy, 52 ds fm NB, for San Francisco; on Abrolhos Banks Dec 7, lat 17 4 lon 37 4, brig Gov. Hopkins, Baker, Dartmouth, 180 sp; 12th, lat 16 57 lon 36 58, barks Exchange, Hazard, NB, clean; 13th, lat 16 30 lon 37, Dr Franklin, Gifford, West-port, 280 sp; bd fm same date, President, Sowle, do, 100 sp on board; Barclay, King, do, 200 sp

Sld fm Greenport 19th, brig Pioneer, (new whaler, 235 tons,) Weeks, S Atlantic Ocean.

At Sydney, N. S. W, in September, ship Harri-son, Sherman, NB, for San Francisco—had shipped her oil to London.

Sld from Zanzibar Oct 10, Phenix, Bloomfield, NL, 120 bbls sp oil; 11th, Columbia, Andrews, do, 240 sp 80 wh.

Sld fm N York Jan 28, steamship Southerner, Berry, Charleston.

Cld at Philadelphia 25th sch Jacob Raymond, Bourne, Charleston.

Ar at Norfolk 22d, sch Bolivar, Barnard, George-town, SC, for this port.

Ship Neptune, of Sagharbor, and Eliza Thornton, of New York, have been purchased in New Bedford, supposed for the California trade.

Letters reed in town from ship Fanny, of this port, for California, rept her, Oct 30, lat 11 41 S, lon 34 09 W, all well.

A letter fm Capt Brush, of ship Golconda, of NB, dated Paita Dec 16, states that he had nearly recov-ered his health, and would leave in a short time for Callao, to rejoin his ship, which was then cruising in charge of the mate.

A letter fm Capt Little, of ship Emma C Jones of NB, repts her at Fayal Dec 17, with 191 bbls sp oil, to be shipped home.

A letter fm Mr. Wm P. Grinnell, dated on board bark Pantheon, Price, NB, at sea, Dec 18, lat 24 N, lon 28 W, all well on board, for San Francisco.

SPOKEN.

At sea, Nov 19, no lat &c., bark John A. Robb, Wimpenny, Fi, for Pacific Ocean, all well.

July 20, lat 37 1-2 lon 74, brig Rodman, Bowen, fm NB, via N York, for Rio Grande and California.

DISASTERS.

Ship Vicksburg, Berry, from New Orleans, at New York, reports Jan 25, at 3.30 A M, Sandy Hook bearing NNW 60 miles, came in contact with the propeller Sea Gull from New York for California—carrying away all our head yards, main yard and fore-top gallant mast; tearing away the larboard fore channels, fore shrouds and foretopmast backstays, staving in rail and breaking several stanchions; also to e away lower standing sail and boom, and split foretopsail and mainsail all to pieces.

Propeller Sea Gull, C essey, from New York for California, on the 25 h, at 4 o'clock in the morning, when 65 miles SE of the Hook was run into by the ship Vicksburg, the Sea Gull being on the wind at the time, which carried away the Sea Gull's three topmasts, head of the main and foremasts, mainyard main topsail, and all the rigging attached; carried away bowsprit, jibboom, stove in larboard bow from the cat head to the fore rigging and down to the plank shear. The Sea Gull was towed to New York, 26th inst, to repair damages.

Telegraphic reports from New Orleans, to the 24th inst, state that the steamer Ohio, from Havana, whilst going up the river, came in collision with the

NOTICE TO MARINERS.
NEW LIGHT HOUSE.

On and after the 1st day of February, 1850, there will be shown from Sankaty Head, on the S. E. part of the Island of NANTUCKET, a new Light, bearing South by West twenty three miles from the Light Vessel on Pollock Rip, and South by East nine miles from the fixed White Light on the extremity of Great Point, Nantucket.

The NEW LIGHT will be a FIXED WHITE LIGHT WITH BRILLIANT WHITE FLASHES: two succes-sive flashes being given at intervals of one and a half minute, then the third flash at an interval of three minutes, followed by two successive flashes at inter-vals of one and a half minute, then a third flash at an interval of three minutes as before, and so on for the time that the Light is visible. The FIXED Light will not be visible farther than 12 or 15 miles, beyond which the flashes only will be seen.

The Light is projected by a revolving Lenticular Ap. aratus of the 2d order.

The centre of the Light will be 15 feet above the level of the sea, and the FLASHES will be visible as far as this elevation and the state of atm spheric re-fraction permit.

The Light Tower is 70 feet high from base to top of Lantern, and will be painted in three rings hori-zontally: the top and bottom rings being white, the middle ring red.

WM. R. EASTON, Collector.
Nantucket, Dec. 24th, 1849.—tF1

GREAT BARGAINS
IN DRY GOODS.
SELLING OFF AT COST, FOR CASH.
JAMES C. CONGDON,

WISHING to close up his present business offers for sale his entire stock of Goods at Cost; consisting in part of Broadcloths, Cassi-meres, Vestings, Rob Roy Plaids, Bleached and Brown Cottons, Bosoms, Collars, Suspenders, Elastic Stocks, Black Kid, White Silk and Wool-len Gloves, Umbrellas, Hose and half Hose, Un-dershirts and Drawers, Silk and Cotton Handker-chiefs, Alpaccas, &c., &c.

LIKEWISE,
Out-Fitting Goods, such as Beaver and Pilot Cloths; Vermont Cassimeres and Satinetts; Ducks, Striped Shirtings, Flannels, Kerseys, Calicoes, for Seamen's fancy Shirts; Blankets, Sheath Knives and Belts, Palms, Jack Knives, Razors, Scissors, Shave Boxes and Brushes.

☞ READY MADE CLOTHING —Over-coats; Sacks; blue and green Jackets, Pants and Vests; Overalls; White Shirts; and many other things too numerous to mention. Also, a beauti-ful lot of Tweed Cloths, suitable for Boys' outside Coats and Sacks.

☞ A splendid assortment of Cloths for Gen-tlemen's Overcoats, Sacks, Dress and Frock Coats, Pants and Vests, together with all other ar-ticles usually kept in Merchant Tailors' Establish-ments.

The above goods are all perfect. All those that have a little money and want a good Garment, will do well to call before purchasing elsewhere. Gen-